Surrendered

Lay it all down... and know the King like never before

9 And whenever the living creatures give glory, honor, and thanks to Him who sits on the throne, to Him who lives forever and ever,

10 the twenty-four elders will **fall down** before Him who sits on the throne, and they will worship Him who lives forever and ever, **and will cast their crowns before the throne**, saying,

11 "Worthy are You, our Lord and our God, to receive glory, honor, and power; for You created all things, and because of Your will they existed, and were created."

Revelation 4:9–11

Scripture quotations have been taken from the NASB 1995, NBLA, and other versions.
This book was created to show biblical principles in a clear, deep, and practical way. It is not intended to replace personal Bible reading and study, but to inspire a closer and more consistent relationship with God through His Word.

First edition: 2025
ISBN: 979-8-9927393-3-6

Visit our website and download the free eBook
A Legacy of Faith: A Powerful Call to Disciple the Next Generation.
JESUSPINKYPROMISE.COM

Leslie Torres
Author

Illustrator:
Amanda Middleton
Behance.net/amandamiddleton

If this devotional has been a blessing to your family, we kindly ask you to leave a five-star review and recommend it to others. By doing so, you help us fulfill the Great Commission, spreading God's Word and blessing more children with His promises.

Together, we can make a difference!

Follow us on social media:

Dear Sister in Christ,

You are not here by accident. If you're holding this book in your hands, it's because the King is calling you to more. More of His presence. More depth. More truth. More intimacy with Him.

This devotional was born from a deep longing the Lord placed in my heart. I long to see women fully surrendered to Him, not just in theory, but in daily practice.

Women who lay down their dreams and desires to embrace the dreams God has for them. Women who are not satisfied with a superficial relationship but dare to give everything for the One who gave everything for them, longing to know Him like never before.

The Word says: "You will seek Me and find Me when you search for Me with all your heart." (Jeremiah 29:13)

That is exactly what this devotional will invite you to do: to seek Him with all your heart.

Over the next 60 days, I invite you to walk with me on a journey of transformation. Every reflection was written with prayer, with struggle, and above all, with hope. You won't find sweet words meant to inspire for just a moment. You'll discover truths that confront, heal, transform, and build you up.

God doesn't want just a part of you. He wants all of you: your soul, spirit, and body, as a living offering.

"Present your bodies as a living and holy sacrifice, acceptable to God, which is your spiritual service of worship." (Romans 12:1)

My prayer is that on every page, you will hear the voice of the King speaking directly to you, drawing you to surrender more and more until your whole life becomes an offering to Him.

If you are ready to know the Lord truly...

Dare to surrender. He is waiting for you.

"Draw near to God, and He will draw near to you." (James 4:8a)

Contents

Week 1: Total Surrender

- Surrender control
- Remember you're not alone
- Walk in your identity in Christ
- Obey and you'll see His hand
- Guard your heart with intention
- Believe even when you can't see
- Master your emotions

Week 2: Fellowship and Relationships

- Fill yourself with His word every day
- Grow in patience
- Whole and undivided
- Walk in His grace
- Even if I lose everything
- Believe that God will make a way
- Cry out with confidence

Week 3: Spiritual Strength

- Surrender to the Transformation of His Word
- Rest without guild in His presence
- Your story has an eternal purpose
- Practice humility every day
- Cultivate a grateful heart
- Remember who fights for you
- Strengthen your soul with the joy of the Lord

Week 4: Inner Healing

- Trust in God's perfect timing
- Do everything in love, even the hard things
- Worship even when you don't understand
- Wait with active hope
- Be brave, stand for your faith
- Renew your mind with the truth
- Live in holiness intentionally

Week 5 –Spiritual Growth

- Embrace silence as spiritual training
- Share your testimony without fear
- Activate a mountain-moving faith
- Respond when He calls you by name
- Break free from the past once and for all
- Stop comparing yourself, you are unique in Him
- Take refuge in the presence of God

Week 6 – Spiritual Power

- Practice disciplines that strengthen you
- Guard your heart from every distraction
- Be an active part of the body of Christ
- Do not improvise: seek anointing with commitment
- Walk with eternal purpose
- Let His power be perfected in your weakness
- Let brokenness transform you

Week 7 – Godly Character

- Do everything with excellence for Him
- shine with the light of Christ wherever you are
- surrender fully to His will
- Let Him heal your deepest wounds
- Believe in the God of the impossible
- Pray with spiritual authority
- Use His word as your sword

Week 8 – Peace and Trust

- Seek restoration, not just to win arguments
- Be a wise and prudent woman
- Love as Christ loves you
- Cultivate a gentle spirit that stands firm in truth
- Live the fruit of the Spirit every day
- Build a life of constant prayer
- Manage your time with eternal intention

Week 9 – Impact and Multiplication

- Obey even when you don't understand
- Receive peace that surpasses all understanding
- Clothe yourself with strength and dignity
- Multiply what God has given you and impact generations

Total Surrender

Surrender Control

Do you struggle to let go of the desire to have everything under control? You're not alone. Many times, we try to manage our circumstances, protect ourselves from pain, or force certain outcomes as if that could guarantee our safety. We convince ourselves that if we plan enough, avoid mistakes, and keep everything "in order," then everything will go well. But that need for control often comes from fear, not faith.

The truth is that the control we think we have is just an illusion. Only YAHWEH has the power, wisdom, and perfect vision to guide our lives. He sees what you cannot see. He knows tomorrow. That's why, as Proverbs reminds us, we are called to trust in the Lord with all our heart and not lean on our own understanding. We must acknowledge Him in all our ways and trust that He will make our paths straight (Proverbs 3:5–6).

When you truly trust, you hand over the wheel. You let go of anxiety, perfectionism, and frustration, and begin to walk in peace, knowing that God is in control. Jesus Himself showed us this path when He prayed in Gethsemane, "Father, if it is possible, let this cup pass from Me. Yet not as I will, but as You will" (Matthew 26:39).
Surrendering control is not weakness. It is spiritual courage. It means recognizing that His will is better, even when you do not understand it. It means letting go of the temporary to embrace the eternal. Philippians encourages us, "Be anxious for nothing... and the peace of God, which surpasses all understanding, will guard your hearts" (Philippians 4:6–7). Today, take a pause. Ask the Lord, "What am I trying to control that I need to surrender to You?" Then give it to Him. His peace is waiting on the other side of surrender.

Prayer
Heavenly Father, I recognize that many times I have tried to take control of my life, my emotions, my relationships, and my plans. Forgive me for trusting in myself more than in You. Today I surrender completely. I give You every burden, every fear, and every attempt to take control. I want to walk in obedience and rest, knowing that You care for me. Direct my steps according to Your will, and fill my heart with the peace that only You can give.
In the name of the Lord Jesus Christ,
Amen.

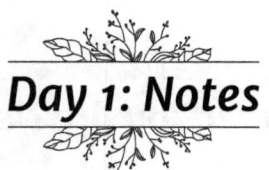

Day 1: Notes

Date: _____

_____

_____

_____

_____

_____

_____

_____

_____

_____

_____

_____

_____

_____

Remember You Are Not Alone

When difficulties pile up or our strength begins to fade, loneliness can become one of the strongest temptations of the heart. We feel that no one understands what we are going through, that our struggle is invisible, that we are walking alone. But that is a lie the enemy wants you to believe to weaken your faith. The truth is, you are never alone. God has promised to always be with you always.

Not only when everything is going well, but especially in the midst of pain, confusion, and exhaustion. His presence is closer than your very breath. He says, "Do not fear, for I am with you. Do not be dismayed, for I am your God. I will strengthen you, I will help you, I will uphold you with My righteous right hand" (Isaiah 41:10).

He is not only with you. He also fights for you. He lifts you when you fall, dries your tears, and sustains your soul when you feel like you can't go on. Jesus Himself promised, "And behold, I am with you always, even to the end of the age" (Matthew 28:20b).

That promise is yours today. It doesn't matter if others have let you down or if you feel invisible, misunderstood, or weak. His faithfulness remains firm. As Scripture declares, "He will never leave you nor forsake you" (Deuteronomy 31:6b).

So today, even if you don't feel anything, choose to believe by faith that He is by your side. Talk to Him, seek His face, and let His love surround you. The God who never fails is with you.

Prayer
Beloved Father, thank You because You are always with me. Forgive me for the times I have felt alone and forgotten Your promise to be by my side. Today I choose to trust in Your constant presence and in Your faithfulness. I ask You to fill me with courage and peace, knowing that You will never leave me. Guide my steps and strengthen my heart.
In the name of the Lord Jesus Christ,
Amen.

Day 2: Notes

Date: _____

_____

_____

_____

_____

_____

_____

_____

_____

_____

_____

_____

_____

_____

_____

Walk in Your Identity in Christ

We live in a world that constantly bombards us with conflicting messages about who we are. Social media, cultural expectations, comparisons, and even our insecurities can cloud our vision of identity. We allow ourselves to be defined by our achievements, failures, appearance, or past. But none of these things has the authority to say who you are.

The Word of God reveals your identity in Christ. You are not what the world labels you. You are not your emotions or your wounds. You are a daughter of the King, created in His image, redeemed by the blood of the Lamb, and loved with an eternal love that the human mind cannot fully comprehend. Scripture declares, "If anyone is in Christ, he is a new creation. The old things have passed away; behold, new things have come" (2 Corinthians 5:17).

From the moment you accepted Christ, your identity was completely transformed. The old you was left behind. You are no longer a slave to guilt, rejection, or the fears of your past. You have been clothed in righteousness, and your name is written in heaven. Only Christ has the right to define who you are. Ephesians reminds us that God chose us in Him before the foundation of the world, that we would be holy and blameless before Him. In love, He predestined us for adoption as His children through Jesus Christ (Ephesians 1:4–5).

Today, choose to believe this truth. Don't walk another day as someone who doesn't know to whom she belongs. Your identity is sealed by the One who cannot lie. You are a daughter. You are loved. You are free.

Prayer
Heavenly Father, thank You for making me Your daughter and for giving me a new identity in Christ. Forgive me for the times I've allowed the world or my insecurities to define who I am. Today, I choose to walk in the identity You have given me, loved, chosen, and renewed. Help me live according to Your truth and always remember that I am Your daughter and that in You, I have everything I need.
In the name of the Lord Jesus Christ,
Amen.

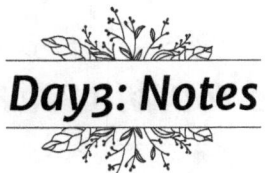

Day3: Notes

Date: _____

_____

_____

_____

_____

_____

_____

_____

_____

_____

_____

_____

_____

_____

Obey and You Will See His Hand

Obedience is one of the most powerful principles in the Christian life. Many times, we want to follow our path, do things our way, and rely on our logic, emotions, or past experiences. But there is only one safe path: the one God lays out through His Word.

Obeying is not always easy. Sometimes it means letting go of what we want, waiting when we would rather move forward, or acting when we would prefer to stay still. Even so, obedience is the language of true love toward God. It's not about following empty rules, but about responding in faith to the voice of the Father, who always knows what is best for us. As Samuel said, "Has the Lord as much delight in burnt offerings and sacrifices as in obeying the voice of the Lord? Behold, to obey is better than sacrifice" (1 Samuel 15:22).

God is not impressed by appearances. He looks for surrendered hearts, ready to listen and follow His lead with humility. Sincere obedience is worth more than any outward display of devotion. In Deuteronomy we read, "If you diligently obey the Lord your God... all these blessings will come upon you and overtake you"
(Deuteronomy 28:1–2).

When you obey, you not only honor God, but you activate His promises in your life. He takes care of the outcome. Jesus Himself modeled this when He said, "If you keep My commandments, you will remain in My love" (John 15:10). Obedience is not just an act of true worship. It is a pathway to intimacy with Christ. It transforms us, strengthens us, and connects us with His heart.

Today, choose to obey, even when you do not understand. The Lord sees your faith and will honor your decision.

Prayer
Heavenly Father, thank You for teaching me the importance of obedience. Forgive me for the times I have wanted to follow my path instead of trusting Your direction. Today I choose to obey Your voice, knowing that Your plans for me are better than mine. Help me walk in Your ways with faith and see Your hand move powerfully in my life. In the name of the Lord Jesus Christ,
Amen.

Day 4: Notes

Date: _____

_____

_____

_____

_____

_____

_____

_____

_____

_____

_____

_____

_____

_____

_____

Guard Your Heart with Intention

The heart is much more than a symbol of emotions. In the Bible, it represents the center of our being. It is the place where thoughts, decisions, desires, and motivations are formed.

That's why it is no surprise that God calls us to guard it with intention, because what happens in the heart determines the direction of our lives. Proverbs tells us clearly, "Above all else, guard your heart, for from it flow the springs of life" (Proverbs 4:23). This is not optional advice; it is a spiritual urgency.

The enemy also wants to occupy that space. He tries to fill it with fear, anxiety, pride, bitterness, jealousy, and hopelessness, often in subtle ways, through distractions or unhealed wounds.

Jesus explained that where your treasure is, there your heart will be also (Matthew 6:21). Whatever we value most, what fills our thoughts and consumes our time, ends up shaping the depths of our soul. If our priorities are out of order, our hearts will inevitably drift away from the path of peace God desires for us.

That is why the Lord gives us a clear strategy for spiritual protection. Philippians encourages us to dwell on whatever is true, honorable, right, pure, and lovely (Philippians 4:8), because our thoughts feed our hearts. We need to train our minds to focus on what builds up and glorifies God. Only then will we find direction and peace, even during chaos.

Today, take an honest look within. What are you allowing into your heart? What thoughts are you feeding? Guard your heart like the treasure it is, because from it flows either life or death.

Prayer
Beloved Father, thank You for reminding me how important it is to guard my heart with intention. Forgive me for the times I have allowed negative thoughts, bitterness, or fear to affect my life. Today I choose to protect my heart and focus my thoughts on what is pure, honorable, and worthy of You. Help me live with a clean heart, fully aligned with Your will. In the name of the Lord Jesus Christ, Amen.

Day 5: Notes

Date: _____

_____

_____

_____

_____

_____

_____

_____

_____

_____

_____

_____

_____

Believe Even When You Don't See It

Faith is not always easy, especially when we don't see immediate results or when our prayers seem unanswered. We live in a culture that values evidence, visible results, and logical explanations. But the Kingdom of God works differently. In His Kingdom, we believe first, and then we see.

Believing in the unseen is a deep act of trust in the character of God. It means trusting not only in what He can do, but in who He is. His faithfulness, His goodness, and His sovereignty never change, even when our circumstances do. "Now faith is the certainty of things hoped for, a proof of things not seen." (Hebrews 11:1)

Faith is not a hopeful wish. It is a spiritual certainty. It is a conviction that comes from knowing God intimately. When you trust His Word, even if you don't understand the process, your heart is filled with peace. "For we walk by faith, not by sight." (2 Corinthians 5:7)

Believing doesn't mean ignoring reality. It means submitting it to a greater truth. The truth is that God is working, even when you cannot see it. Sometimes His answer is not what we expected, but it is always what we need. That is where faith matures: when we rest in His will more than in our desires.

Jesus said to Thomas,
"Because you have seen Me, have you now believed? Blessed are they who did not see, and yet believed." (John 20:29)

Today, choose to believe even if you don't see. Believe that God is moving, that His timing is perfect, and that His promises will not fail.

Prayer
Heavenly Father, help me believe even when I don't see. Forgive me for the times I have doubted or allowed my circumstances to shake my faith. Today I choose to trust You and Your promises, knowing that what I cannot see with my natural eyes, I will see through the eyes of faith. Thank You for always being with me and guiding my steps.
In the name of the Lord Jesus Christ,
Amen.

Day 6: Notes

Date: _____

_____

_____

_____

_____

_____

_____

_____

_____

_____

_____

_____

_____

_____

_____

Master Your Emotions

Emotions are a gift from God, but they were not meant to rule our lives. They are signals, not drivers. We may feel anger, sadness, fear, or frustration, but we must not allow those emotions to take control of our decisions or actions. The Christian life is about learning to live guided by the Spirit, not by the impulses of the soul.

"Like a city that is broken into and without walls is a man who has no control over his spirit." (Proverbs 25:28)

A city without walls is vulnerable to any attack. That is what a person without emotional control is like. They are quick to react instead of responding, easily offended, constantly anxious, or prone to outbursts of anger. But the Holy Spirit offers us something greater: self-control, a visible fruit of a surrendered life. "But the fruit of the Spirit is... self-control." (Galatians 5:22–23)

Self-control is not repression. It is freedom. It is the power to choose how to respond. And one of the areas where we need it most is in forgiveness. Being overly sensitive to offense steals our peace. Jesus taught us to pray for our enemies, to forgive seventy times seven, and to trust that God is the one who fights our battles.

"Be anxious for nothing... and the peace of God... will guard your hearts and minds."
(Philippians 4:6–7)

When we surrender our emotions to the Lord, His peace replaces the chaos. He not only calms the storms around us but also the ones within us.

Today, choose to master your emotions. Don't let anger, anxiety, or bitterness rule your life. Surrender everything to God and allow the Spirit to lead you with wisdom and peace.

Prayer

Heavenly Father, thank You for giving me the power to master my emotions through the Holy Spirit. Forgive me for the times I've allowed my emotions to control me and pull me away from Your peace. Today I choose to submit my thoughts and feelings to You. Help me respond with wisdom and self-control, trusting that You will guide my heart and mind in every moment. I also ask that You give me a forgiving heart and help me not be led by offense. In the name of the Lord Jesus Christ,
Amen.

Day 7: Notes

Date: _____

_____

_____

_____

_____

_____

_____

_____

_____

_____

_____

_____

_____

_____

Fellowship and Relationships

Fill Yourself with His Word Every Day

The Word of God is our source of life, wisdom, and strength. If we want to live with peace, purpose, and direction, we need to immerse ourselves in it daily. Jesus taught us that man shall not live by bread alone, but by every word that comes from the mouth of God (Matthew 4:4).

The Bible is not just a book of stories. It is the living and active Word of God, with the power to transform our lives. Through it, we come to know His heart and His character.

Psalm 119:105 says: "Your word is a lamp to my feet and a light to my path." The Word lights our path when everything seems dark. It gives us clarity when facing difficult decisions, guides us when we feel lost, and directs us in times of uncertainty.

It is a lamp that allows us to move forward with confidence, knowing we are following His will.

Paul wrote in 2 Timothy 3:16–17: "All Scripture is inspired by God and beneficial for teaching, for rebuke, for correction, for training in righteousness…"

The Bible teaches, corrects, and instructs us to live according to God's will. It is a manual for a life that honors Him, builds us up, and prepares us for every good work. Jesus also said: "If you continue in My word… you will know the truth, and the truth will set you free." (John 8:31–32) The Word not only guides. It also sets us free. It frees us from lies, confusion, and sin. It enables us to live in freedom, according to His truth.

Today, make Bible reading a priority. Filling yourself with His Word will give you peace, direction, and draw you closer to the heart of God.

Prayer

Beloved Father, thank You for giving us Your Word, which is living, powerful, and faithful. Help me seek You each day through it, to find guidance during confusion and strength in times of weariness. Teach me to love the Scriptures, to obey them, and to live according to Your truth. I want to know You more and allow Your Word to transform my heart. In the name of Jesus Christ,
Amen.

Day 8: Notes

Date: _____

_____

_____

_____

_____

_____

_____

_____

_____

_____

_____

_____

_____

_____

Grow in Patience

Patience is a virtue that is often tested in difficult moments. We live in a culture of instant gratification, but God desires for us to cultivate patience. It's not just about waiting calmly, but about trusting that He is in control and working at the perfect time.

James 5:7–8 says: "Therefore be patient, brothers and sisters, until the coming of the Lord. See how the farmer waits for the precious fruit... waiting patiently... You too be patient; strengthen your hearts..."
Just as the farmer waits for the fruit, knowing the process takes time, our spiritual life also requires patience. God is at work in us, even when we don't see immediate results.

Romans 12:12 reminds us: "Rejoicing in hope, persevering in tribulation, devoted to prayer." Patience is strengthened through tribulation. It's natural to want quick solutions, but learning to wait on God develops character, faith, and deeper dependence on Him.

Second Peter 3:9 says: "The Lord is not slow about His promise... but is patient... not wanting anyone to perish..." God is patient with us. His patience is a model that teaches us that seasons of waiting have purpose. He is never late.

Today, choose to grow in patience. In every moment of waiting or difficulty, remember that God is working. Patience prepares you, shapes you, and makes you more like Christ.

Prayer
Heavenly Father, thank You for Your patience with me. Forgive me for the times I have tried to rush Your timing and lost my peace. Today I choose to trust You and be patient in moments of waiting. Help me remember that You are in control and that everything You do has a perfect purpose. I ask You to strengthen my patience and teach me to wait with hope, knowing that You are never late. In the name of the Lord Jesus Christ,
Amen.

Day 9: Notes

Date: _____

_____

_____

_____

_____

_____

_____

_____

_____

_____

_____

_____

_____

_____

Whole and Undivided

The Christian life is not about separate actions, but about living with consistency and unity. God calls us to be whole in Him. He wants us to live according to what we believe and reflect His love in every area of our lives. Living "whole and undivided" means being authentic and sincere with ourselves and others, without separating our faith from our actions.

In 1 Thessalonians 5:23–24, we read:

"Now may the God of peace Himself sanctify you entirely; and may your spirit and soul and body be kept complete, without blame at the coming of our Lord Jesus Christ. Faithful is He who calls you, and He also will do it."

God desires to sanctify us completely in every part of our being: spirit, soul, and body. We cannot live a partial faith, applying it only to spiritual matters while ignoring our emotions, thoughts, or decisions. Every part of us should reflect Christ.

James 1:8 warns:

"A double-minded man is unstable in all his ways."

When our actions and beliefs are aligned, we live with purpose. But when there is division in our hearts, we become unstable and lose the clarity God wants to give us.

Colossians 3:17 says:

"Whatever you do in word or deed, do everything in the name of the Lord Jesus..."

To live with integrity means that every word and action reflects Christ. It's not about being perfect, but about surrendering every area of our lives to Him.

Today, take a moment to reflect. Are there areas of your life that are not aligned with God? Ask Him to transform you and help you live with integrity. Be honest, steady, and fully transparent before Him.

Prayer

Heavenly Father, thank You for calling me to live a consistent and complete life in You. Forgive me for the times I've divided my life between what I believe and what I do. Today I choose to live with integrity, allowing my life to reflect Your love and will always. Help me be sincere with myself and with others, and to live according to Your truth in every area of my life. In the name of the Lord Jesus Christ, Amen.

Day 10: Notes

Date: _____

_____

_____

_____

_____

_____

_____

_____

_____

_____

_____

_____

_____

Walk in His Grace

There are days when our strength simply isn't enough. Days when exhaustion, guilt, past mistakes, or the voices around us make us feel useless or not enough. But God's grace is not based on what you can accomplish. It is based on what Christ already accomplished for you. The apostle Paul wrote that the Lord said to him:
"My grace is sufficient for you, for power is perfected in weakness."
And then he concluded:
"Most gladly, therefore, I will rather boast about my weaknesses, so that the power of Christ may dwell in me."
(2 Corinthians 12:9)

Walking in His grace is not an excuse to settle for a mediocre life. It is an invitation to live in freedom, fully depending on His power. His grace not only saves us; it transforms us, sustains us, and reminds us that we don't need to impress God. What we need is to surrender to Him. When we walk in His grace, we stop carrying a weight that was never ours to carry. We acknowledge that yes, we are weak, but that is exactly where His power is made perfect. We stop comparing ourselves to other women. We stop demanding perfection from ourselves. And we begin to enjoy the freedom of being led by the Holy Spirit.

Walking in His grace also means accepting that not everything depends on us. It is resting in His faithfulness, trusting His daily guidance, and remembering that even when we fall, His grace lifts us again and again. It is living with the awareness that His love is not based on our performance, but on His unchanging character.
Stop walking on your strength. Walk in His grace, one step at a time, trusting that He is holding your hand.

Prayer
Father, thank You for Your grace that never runs out. Forgive me for the days when I tried to do everything on my own. Today I choose to walk in Your grace, not because I have to, but because I know that in my weakness, Your power is made perfect. Help me let go of guilt, pride, and self-sufficiency. Teach me to depend completely on You. In the name of Jesus Christ,
Amen.

Day 11: Notes

Date: _____

_____

_____

_____

_____

_____

_____

_____

_____

_____

_____

_____

_____

_____

Even If I Lose Everything

Job lost everything, yet he worshiped. During his pain, he humbly declared, "Naked I came from my mother's womb, and naked I shall return there. The Lord gave and the Lord has taken away. Blessed be the name of the Lord." (Job 1:21)

Daniel's friends faced the fiery furnace, but they stood firm. They responded to the king with unshakable conviction: "Our God whom we serve is able to rescue us... but even if He does not, let it be known to you, O king, that we are not going to serve your gods." (Daniel 3:17–18)

Esther risked her life to obey God's purpose, and with courage she said, "I will go into the king, even though it is not according to the law. And if I perish, I perish." (Esther 4:16)

In each of these stories, there is an invisible but powerful thread. It is a kind of faith that does not depend on the outcome, a trust that does not break even when everything goes wrong.

As Christian women, we must learn to embrace this unshakable faith. God never promised us a life without trials. His Word tells us that in this world, we will face afflictions. Faith is not about getting what we want. It is about remaining faithful, even if we receive nothing.

Toxic feminism has tried to convince us that we are enough on our own, that we can handle everything, and that we don't need anyone. But that is not what the Bible teaches. We were not created to be self-sufficient. We were created to depend on our Creator. And when we embrace that truth, we become truly free.

Our faith must be anchored in what is eternal, not in what is temporary. Even if we lose everything here, we have already gained what is most valuable: God's promise of eternal life with our Lord.

Prayer

Heavenly Father, thank You for showing us through the lives of Job, Daniel, and Esther that it is worth standing firm, even when things don't go as we hoped. Teach us to live with a content heart, trusting that we already have what matters most: God's promise of eternal life. Deliver us from the lie of feminism that tries to make us believe we can do it all on our own. I am not enough, and that's okay because I have Christ. Through Him, I can come near to You. May my faith not depend on results, but on who You are. In the name of Jesus Christ, Amen.

Day 12: Notes

Date: _____

_____

_____

_____

_____

_____

_____

_____

_____

_____

_____

_____

_____

_____

Believe That God Will Make a Way

There are moments when we feel like there's no way out. The situation seems closed on every side, like we're standing in front of a sea we cannot cross. But God doesn't need the way to be open to act. He is the One who makes a way. He is the Way.

This is what He declared in Isaiah: "This is what the Lord says: He who makes a way through the sea and a path through the mighty waters." (Isaiah 43:16)

And He didn't just say it. He proved it. When the people of Israel were trapped between the Egyptian army and the Red Sea, God didn't ask them for a strategy, only obedience. He stretched out His hand and parted the sea in two. The impossible became a way forward.

That same God is the One who walks with you today. Maybe you're in the middle of a desert, unsure of which way to go. Maybe you've been praying for a long time without seeing an answer, and you've started to wonder if God is silent or if He has forgotten you.

But listen to what He promises: "Behold, I am doing something new... I will make a roadway in the wilderness, rivers in the desert." (Isaiah 43:19)

God is not limited by your circumstances. He doesn't need ideal conditions to act. All He needs is a heart that trusts Him. Even if you don't see it yet, He is already working behind the scenes. Even when you don't understand, you can rest knowing that nothing is outside of His control.

Believe. Not because everything is going right, but because He said so. He fulfills what He promises. His power has no limits, and His faithfulness never fails. Where you see an ending, God sees a new beginning.

Have faith. God will make a way.

Prayer

Father, thank You for being the God who makes a way through the sea and brings rivers to life in the desert. Help me trust when I don't understand, to wait with hope, and to walk in obedience even when I can't see the way out. I believe in Your faithfulness and Your promises. I know that You will make a way. In the name of Jesus Christ, Amen.

Day 13: Notes

Date: _____

_____

_____

_____

_____

_____

_____

_____

_____

_____

_____

_____

_____

Cry Out with Confidence

God is not bothered when you cry out to Him. He is not uncomfortable with your tears, your questions, or your moments of desperation. On the contrary, His Word invites us again and again to come to Him with freedom and confidence.
"Call to Me and I will answer you, and I will tell you great and mighty things, which you do not know."
(Jeremiah 33:3)

When you cry out to God with confidence, you're not shouting into the air. You're calling on the Father who loves you, who hears you, and who moves with compassion on behalf of His daughters. He doesn't just listen. He responds. Maybe not in the way you expected or at the time you wished, but His answer is always perfect, and His faithfulness never fails.

Sometimes it's hard to cry out because we feel guilty, unworthy, or because we think we've already prayed too much. But our God is not like us. He is patient, slow to anger, and rich in mercy. Don't stop crying out. Don't stop talking to Him. Don't hold back what's hurting you.

Hebrews 4:16 reminds us:
"Therefore, let's approach the throne of grace with confidence, so that we may receive mercy and find grace for help at the time of our need."

You can come with boldness, not because of who you are, but because of what Christ did for you. You have direct access to the throne of the King. So why stay silent when you can cry out?

Prayer
Father, thank You for hearing me every time I cry out to You. Forgive me when I doubt or when I pull away out of fear or guilt. Today I come with confidence, not because of my merit, but because of Christ's work. I pour out my heart before You, trusting that You see me, hear me, and will respond according to Your perfect will.
In the name of Jesus Christ,
Amen.

Day 14: Notes

Date: _____

_____

_____

_____

_____

_____

_____

_____

_____

_____

_____

_____

_____

_____

_____

_____

Spiritual Strength

Surrender to the Transformation of His Word

Reading the Bible is not just a spiritual practice. It is a constant transformation. The Word of God was not written to simply inform you but to form you. When you open the Scriptures with a willing heart, you will not stay the same.

"For the word of God is living and active, and sharper than any two-edged sword..." (Hebrews 4:12)

It penetrates, heals, corrects, and renews. It is not dead ink; it is a living voice.

But for that transformation to happen, it's not enough to read out of routine or obligation. We need to come with humility, recognizing that there are areas in our lives that must be aligned with God's will. His Word is the mirror that reveals who we are, but also the tool that shapes us to be more like Christ.

Sometimes that confrontation can be painful, because truth, when it shines into darkness, can be uncomfortable. But there is no growth without discomfort. There is no maturity without correction. That's why Paul wrote: "All Scripture is inspired by God and beneficial for teaching, for rebuke, for correction, for training in righteousness." (2 Timothy 3:16)

Letting His Word transform you means surrendering your heart daily. It means having a teachable spirit and allowing God to deal with the deepest parts of your character. It is saying, "Lord, I don't want to read just to know more about You. I want to read to become more like You."

Let every verse be a seed of change. Let every reading be a conversation with the One who loves you too much to leave you the same. And may His Word find fertile ground in you, ready to bear fruit for His glory.

Prayer

Father, thank You for Your holy, living, and powerful Word. Today I surrender to it. I want to be transformed from the depths of my being. Remove anything that does not please You. Correct what is crooked. Plant in me a passion for Your truth. Speak to me as I read and help me obey what You reveal. In the name of Jesus Christ, Amen.

Day 15: Notes

Date: _____

_____

_____

_____

_____

_____

_____

_____

_____

_____

_____

_____

_____

_____

Rest Without Guilt in His Presence

We live in a culture that celebrates constant productivity, where slowing down is often seen as laziness or a lack of commitment. But God did not design you to live exhausted. He calls you to rest, not just physically, but also spiritually and emotionally.
"Come to Me, all who are weary and burdened, and I will give you rest." (Matthew 11:28)

True rest is found in His presence. It's not inactivity; it's intimacy. It's allowing your soul to breathe, your heart to align with God's rhythm, and your mind to be freed from the noise of the world. Sometimes, even when we try to rest, we do so with guilt, as if stopping were a sign of weakness or irresponsibility.

But resting is also obedience.
We need to care for our bodies. Sleeping well, eating wisely, and learning to say "no" when needed are also part of a surrendered life. Even those who serve in ministry must set aside time for renewal to avoid emotional and spiritual burnout.

God doesn't love you for what you do, but for who you are in Christ. He doesn't measure you by your productivity but by your obedience. And part of that obedience is learning to pause and say, "Today I can't do it all, but You can." Rest is a form of surrender. It's acknowledging that we need Him, and that without Him we can do nothing.

Just as Jesus withdrew to be with the Father, you also need those moments. Not to do more, but to remember that your value is in the One to whom you belong.

Prayer
Father, thank You for reminding me that resting is also obedience. Help me let go of guilt, care for my body and soul, and take time with You without distractions. Teach me to set healthy boundaries, enjoy time with my family, and live with balance. In the name of Jesus Christ,
Amen.

Day 16: Notes

Date: _____

_____

_____

_____

_____

_____

_____

_____

_____

_____

_____

_____

_____

_____

Your Story Has an Eternal Purpose

Nothing in your life has been in vain. There is no detail, wound, failure, or season that God cannot use to fulfill His eternal purpose in you. Even what once looked like loss, detour, or shame is being woven into the perfect plan of the One who sees beyond the present.
"And we know that God causes all things to work together for good to those who love God." (Romans 8:28)

Maybe your story didn't start well. Maybe there was abandonment, abuse, sin, or decisions you wish you could erase. But when you surrender your life to Christ, your past is not just left behind, it is redeemed. He doesn't just forgive you. He gives purpose to what once seemed ruined. He turns your story into a living testimony of His grace.

God is not looking for women with perfect stories. He is looking for surrendered hearts, willing to let His light shine through even the darkest chapters.

"God has chosen the foolish things of the world to shame the wise..." (1 Corinthians 1:27) What the enemy meant for destruction, God can use to build, to heal, and to lift others. Every chapter, even the hardest ones, can become evidence of God's power at work in your life.

Your story matters. Don't hide it. Don't be ashamed of what God has already forgiven. There is someone out there who needs to know she's not alone, that there is hope, and that if God did it for you, He can do it for her too.

Prayer
Father, thank You for reminding me that my story has value in Your hands. Even though some parts still hurt, I know You can use them to bless, to heal, and to reveal Your power. Today I surrender every chapter of my life to You, trusting that nothing is wasted when it's in Your hands. Redeem my past, use it for Your glory, and make me a voice of hope for others. In the name of Jesus Christ, Amen.

Day 17: Notes

Date: _____

_____

_____

_____

_____

_____

_____

_____

_____

_____

_____

_____

_____

_____

Practice Humility Every Day

Humility is not weakness; it is strength under control. It is the heart that recognizes its daily need for God. It's not about thinking less of yourself, but thinking of yourself less. It's living with the awareness that everything we are, have, and accomplish comes from Him.

Humility must be practiced. It's not a feeling; it's a daily decision. It's choosing to serve without expecting recognition. It's asking for forgiveness when you're wrong. It's yielding when you could demand your way. It's valuing others above yourself, just as Christ did.
"Have this attitude in yourselves which was also in Christ Jesus... who emptied Himself, taking the form of a bond-servant."
(Philippians 2:5,7)

Humility cannot be forced. It must be cultivated. It is born in intimacy with God when we understand that apart from Him, we can do nothing. A humble woman doesn't need to prove her worth because she knows who she belongs to. Her identity is firmly rooted in Christ.
In a world that promotes pride, self-reliance, and doing things your way, living with humility is a radical act of obedience. But God lifts the humble. He guides them, protects them, and transforms them.
"God is opposed to the proud, but gives grace to the humble."
(James 4:6)

Humility also means admitting that you need help. That you don't have all the answers. That you rely on His grace for every step. When you walk in humility, your heart becomes more sensitive, your character is strengthened, and your life begins to reflect Christ more deeply. And the more you become like Christ, the more naturally you will live in humility, because you will see both His greatness and His gentleness.

Practice humility every day. Not to be seen, but to be transformed.

Prayer
Father, teach me to live with a humble heart. Free me from pride disguised as self-reliance. Help me to depend on You, to value others, and to serve with joy. May the world see less of me and more of Christ in me each day. In the name of Jesus Christ,
Amen.

Day 18: Notes

Date: _____

_____

_____

_____

_____

_____

_____

_____

_____

_____

_____

_____

_____

_____

Cultivate a Grateful Heart

Gratitude doesn't come from having it all, but from recognizing that everything we have is by grace. A grateful heart is not one without problems. It is one that has learned to see God's faithfulness even in the middle of them. "In everything give thanks, for this is the will of God for you in Christ Jesus." (1 Thessalonians 5:18)

Being thankful doesn't mean ignoring the pain or pretending everything is okay. It means choosing to focus on what God has done, is doing, and will do, instead of staying stuck in what you haven't yet seen. "Bless the Lord, my soul, and do not forget any of His benefits." (Psalm 103:2)

Gratitude transforms. It turns complaints into praise, worries into prayers, and scarcity into trust. It teaches us to value what is already present and to live with an eternal perspective.
"Enter His gates with thanksgiving and His courtyards with praise. Give thanks to Him, bless His name." (Psalm 100:4)

A grateful heart becomes strong. Complaining loses its grip. Comparison grows weaker. And instead of living from a place of lack, you begin to live from the abundance of His love.
Gratitude doesn't wait for perfect circumstances. It finds reasons in what is eternal. "Rejoice always. Pray without ceasing. In everything give thanks." (1 Thessalonians 5:16–18)

Gratitude is a spiritual discipline. It grows through truth, prayer, and daily choice. And when you cultivate it, joy begins to bloom, not because of what you have, but because of who you have. In Christ, you have everything.

Prayer
Father, today I choose to give thanks. Not because everything is perfect, but because You are good. Open my eyes to see Your faithfulness in the everyday. Free me from complaining and teach me to live with a heart full of gratitude, trusting that Your love always sustains me. In the name of Jesus Christ,
Amen.

Day 19: Notes

Date: _____

_____

_____

_____

_____

_____

_____

_____

_____

_____

_____

_____

_____

_____

_____

Remember Who Fights for You

When life's battles intensify, it's easy to fall into the temptation of fighting in your strength. We get exhausted, frustrated, and often feel defeated before the real fight has even begun. But there's a truth we need to remember every day: we are not alone in the battle.
"The Lord will fight for you, while you keep silent." (Exodus 14:14)

The enemy wants you to believe that you've been abandoned, that you have no defense, and that it all depends on you. But our victory is not found in our strategies. It is found in our dependence. It's not about keeping everything under control, but about surrendering control to the One who never loses. When you acknowledge your weakness and hand the wheel over to God, He moves in power. He is not a spectator in your struggle. He is your defender, your shield, and your strength.

Throughout the Bible, God showed that He fights for His people. Not because they deserved it, but because He is faithful. He fought for Israel, for David, for Esther, and for many others who dared to trust Him. And today, He is still fighting for you. He is fighting for your home, your heart, your children, and your purpose. He goes before you like a mighty warrior. "Be strong and courageous... for the Lord your God is the one who is going with you. He will not desert you or abandon you." (Deuteronomy 31:6)

Surrendering doesn't mean giving in to defeat. It means yielding to His power. Don't fight alone. Let God fight for you. Take your position in prayer, obedience, and faith. Then watch Him move on your behalf.

Prayer
Father, thank You that I am not alone in my battles. Today I release control and surrender to Your power. Fight for me, Lord. Fight for my home, my heart, and everything that feels too big for me. Teach me to trust that You go before me and that You will never leave me. In the name of Jesus Christ,
Amen.

Day 20: Notes

Date: _____

_____

_____

_____

_____

_____

_____

_____

_____

_____

_____

_____

_____

_____

Strengthen Your Soul with the Joy of the Lord

There are days when emotional and spiritual strength feels completely drained. Worries, bad news, physical exhaustion, and routine can sap every drop of motivation. But God has given us an unending source of renewal: "The joy of the Lord is my strength." (Nehemiah 8:10)

This joy does not depend on favorable circumstances or fleeting emotions. It is a deep certainty that God is with you, that your life is in His hands, and that His purpose will be fulfilled even if you can't see the way right now. The joy of the Lord is not a forced smile or a shallow feeling. It is a steady posture of the heart that says, "He is still good, and that is enough for me."

To strengthen your soul with the joy of the Lord is to choose to look beyond the present moment and rest in God's faithfulness. It is to worship through tears. To give thanks without having all the answers. To declare victory in the middle of the process.
"Though the fig tree does not blossom... yet I will rejoice in the Lord." (Habakkuk 3:17–18)

This kind of joy is born in intimacy with God, in knowing Him, in trusting that He is sovereign even when everything around you feels uncertain. It is not a denial of pain. It is remembering that pain does not have the final word.

Don't look for strength within yourself. Seek the joy that comes from knowing who your God is. Laugh, sing, worship, and rest in Him. Feed your soul with living hope. And you will see how, even on the darkest days, new strength begins to rise from above.

Prayer
Lord, thank You for reminding me that my strength doesn't come from me, but from You. Today I choose to rejoice in Your faithfulness. Even when things don't turn out the way I hope, I find joy in Your presence. Fill my soul with the kind of joy that renews, lifts, and strengthens me. In the name of Jesus Christ,
Amen.

Day 21: Notes

Date: _____

_____

_____

_____

_____

_____

_____

_____

_____

_____

_____

_____

_____

_____

Inner Healing

Trust in God's Perfect Timing

Waiting can be one of the greatest challenges in the Christian life. We want answers now, immediate solutions, and doors to open without delay. But God does not move according to our clock. He operates with perfect timing, and trusting in that is a deep act of faith.
"He has made everything appropriate in its time."
(Ecclesiastes 3:11)

Sometimes it feels like God is taking too long. But the truth is, He is never late. While you are waiting, He is working in places you cannot see. He is preparing your heart, shaping your character, and aligning circumstances so that His will is fulfilled in the right way and at the right moment. Trusting His timing means surrendering your need for control. It is saying, "Lord, I don't understand when, but I trust who." Because the God who made the promise is faithful, and His schedule is not dictated by the world's pressure or our emotions.

The process of waiting also reveals what is in our hearts. It teaches us to depend more, to pray more, and to listen more closely. God does not use time to punish. He uses it to prepare. Sometimes the answer hasn't come yet because our hearts aren't ready to carry what He wants to give us.

Remembering God's past faithfulness will help you wait with active hope. He hasn't failed you before, and He will not fail you now.
"The Lord is not slow about His promise, as some count slowness, but is patient toward you."
(2 Peter 3:9)

His patience is not forgetfulness. It is love.
Rest. You are not wasting time. You are being prepared. And when God's moment comes, you'll know, and everything will fall into place.

Prayer
Lord, help me trust in Your perfect timing. Sometimes I grow impatient, but today I choose to wait in faith. Strengthen my heart as I wait, and don't let anxiety steal my peace. You know what's best, and I trust You. In the name of Jesus Christ,
Amen.

Day 22: Notes

Date: _____

_____

_____

_____

_____

_____

_____

_____

_____

_____

_____

_____

_____

_____

_____

Do Everything with Love, Even the Hard Things

Loving is not always easy. It's often one of the hardest things we are called to do. Loving when you've been hurt, when no one notices, when you're exhausted, or when the situation feels unfair. But if we want to become more like Christ, love is not optional. It is the way. "Let all that you do be done in love." (1 Corinthians 16:14)

True love does not depend on emotions. It is a conscious decision, an attitude of the heart that says, "I do this for the Lord." When you love in the everyday moments, such as serving, correcting, forgiving, or speaking, you reflect the character of God, who loved us first and loves us unconditionally.

Even in the hardest situations, you can choose to act in love. That doesn't mean allowing abuse or staying silent in the face of injustice. Sometimes, love also means setting boundaries. Protecting your heart and well-being is not selfish. It is obedience. In some cases, it is necessary to take distance from those who mistreat or abuse you.

That distance may be temporary, while God heals and restores, or it may be permanent and necessary. But it should always be done without resentment and with a heart that seeks to honor God. Creating space without hatred is also an act of love.
"Love is patient, love is kind... it does not seek its own, is not provoked, does not keep a record of wrongs." (1 Corinthians 13:4–5)

That kind of love is possible when we allow God to produce it in us. When you do everything with love, even your daily tasks become acts of worship. Your words bring healing. Your decisions bring blessings. Your actions plant seeds of eternity. Nothing done in love, in the name of the Lord, is ever in vain.

Prayer
Lord, help me to do everything with love, even when it's hard. Free me from pride, harshness, or indifference. Teach me to love the way You love. Let me love with patience, kindness, and truth. And if I need to set boundaries, help me do it with wisdom, without bitterness, and with a heart firmly rooted in You. In the name of Jesus Christ, Amen.

Day 23: Notes

Date: _____

_____

_____

_____

_____

_____

_____

_____

_____

_____

_____

_____

_____

_____

Worship Even When You Don't Understand

There are moments when we simply don't understand. Prayers go unanswered in the way we hoped. Doors close. Suffering arrives without explanation. And heaven seems silent. In those moments, mature faith learns to worship. Not because of what it sees, but because of who God is. "Then Job got up... fell to the ground and worshiped." (Job 1:20)

Worshiping when everything is going well is beautiful, but worshiping when everything hurts is deep. It is the kind of worship that touches the heart of God. It is praise that flows from total surrender, from a soul that has decided to trust even without understanding. It is the kind of faith that does not need explanations to remain standing, because it has learned that God's presence is enough.

God does not owe us explanations. But He does give us His presence. He may not always reveal the "why," but He always offers the "for what." He uses it to shape us, to show us His faithfulness, to perfect His power in our weakness. When we worship in the middle of confusion, our soul aligns with His will, and our eyes rise above our circumstances.

"Though the fig tree does not blossom... yet I will rejoice in the Lord." (Habakkuk 3:17–18) That is the decision of a surrendered heart. A faith that does not base its worship on results but finds in God Himself the reason to keep singing.

Today, you may not understand what you're going through. But worship anyway. Because He is still worthy. Because He has not changed. Because during your pain, His love remains. And where there is worship, His presence is there.

Prayer

Lord, today I choose to worship You, even when I don't understand. Even if my plans don't turn out the way I hoped, my heart surrenders to You. You are always worthy of praise. Fill my soul with faith and remind me that Your presence is enough. In the name of Jesus Christ, Amen.

Day 24: Notes

Date: _____

_____

_____

_____

_____

_____

_____

_____

_____

_____

_____

_____

_____

_____

_____

Wait with Active Hope

Waiting on God does not mean standing still. Biblical hope is not passive. It is alive. It is a firm expectation based on the faithfulness of a God who does not lie. While you wait for His answer, you can continue sowing, worshiping, serving, and growing.
"The Lord is good to those who wait for Him, to the person who seeks Him." (Lamentations 3:25)

We often associate waiting with inaction, but in the Kingdom of God, waiting is part of the training. It is in that process where faith, patience, and obedience are strengthened. David was anointed as king, but he waited years before taking the throne. During that time, he didn't sit idle. He kept fighting, serving, and honoring God.
"Wait for the Lord. Be strong, and let your heart take courage. Yes, wait for the Lord." (Psalm 27:14)

Active hope is not fed by what it sees but by what it believes. It is an attitude of the heart that says, "I don't have the answer yet, but I will keep walking by faith." You can study, prepare your heart, improve your habits, keep serving in the small things, and pray with perseverance, knowing that God is also working behind the scenes.
"But if we hope for what we do not see, through perseverance we wait eagerly for it." (Romans 8:25)

Waiting is not resignation. It is trust. It is moving forward in faith even without immediate results. It is sowing with tears today, believing the harvest will come in God's perfect time. It is allowing God to shape you in the process, knowing that every day of waiting has an eternal purpose. Don't waste time wishing the wait would end. Use this time to grow. Waiting with purpose produces lasting fruit. And when the promise comes, your heart will be ready to receive it.

Prayer
Lord, thank You for teaching me that waiting is not a waste of time. I want to wait on You with a steady heart and a living hope. Show me what steps to take while I wait, and help me trust that Your work is moving forward, even when I cannot see it. In the name of Jesus Christ,
Amen.

Day 25: Notes

Date: _____

_____

_____

_____

_____

_____

_____

_____

_____

_____

_____

_____

_____

_____

_____

Be Brave, Stand for Your Faith

True faith will not always be popular. We live in a world that celebrates what God calls sin and rejects what He calls holy. Standing for your faith today might mean being judged, ridiculed, or even excluded. But the Lord's call remains the same: "Be strong and courageous. Do not be terrified or dismayed, for the Lord your God is with you wherever you go." (Joshua 1:9)

We are not called to live a comfortable faith, but a courageous one. When you choose to live according to God's Word, you are lifting a torch in the midst of darkness. Not everyone will understand, but God honors those who honor Him. In times like these, we need women who rise with courage, and who are not ashamed of the gospel, because "it is the power of God for salvation to everyone who believes." (Romans 1:16)

Standing for your faith doesn't always require words. More often, it is shown in daily choices—what you watch, what you share, how you respond, and even who you choose to walk with. Biblical courage doesn't come from pride. It comes from the humility of someone who knows whom they have trusted. As the apostle Paul wrote, "For am I now seeking the approval of people, or of God? Or am I striving to please people? If I were still trying to please people, I would not be a bond-servant of Christ." (Galatians 1:10)

Be brave. Even if your voice shakes, speak the truth. Even if there is no applause, live with integrity. Even if it hurts, stand firm. God not only sees your struggle, He fights with you. And when you defend your faith with love and conviction, He strengthens you, restores you, and uses you for His glory.

Prayer
Father, thank You for giving me a faith that is worth defending. Help me be brave and not stay silent out of fear of rejection. May Your Holy Spirit fill me with power, love, and self-control so I can live with integrity and speak the truth. I want to honor You with my choices, my words, and my life. Strengthen me when I feel alone, and remind me that You are always with me. In the name of Jesus Christ, Amen.

Day 26: Notes

Date: _____

_____

_____

_____

_____

_____

_____

_____

_____

_____

_____

_____

_____

Renew Your Mind with the Truth

The thoughts we hold on to have power. They can lead us toward freedom or keep us bound in fear, guilt, or confusion. That is why the Bible calls us to renew our minds, not with motivational phrases, but with the truth of God. "Do not be conformed to this world, but be transformed by the renewing of your mind, so that you may prove what the will of God is, that which is good and acceptable and perfect." (Romans 12:2)

Healing the heart begins by transforming the way we think. Many times, we silently repeat lies. Thoughts like: "I'll never change," "This is too much for me," or "I don't have what it takes." But the truth is that we can't do it on our own, and that's okay. We weren't created to carry the weight alone. Our strength is found through Christ.
"I can do all things through Him who strengthens me."
(Philippians 4:13)

The Lord calls us to tear down every defeated thought that doesn't come from Him. "We are destroying arguments, and all arrogance raised against the knowledge of God, and we are taking every thought captive to the obedience of Christ." (2 Corinthians 10:5)

Renewing your mind takes intention. It's not automatic. It is a daily practice. Every time you choose to believe what God says about you, you are taking spiritual authority over your life. It doesn't matter how many times you've failed. What matters is what He says about you, that you are forgiven, chosen, loved, and equipped to walk in freedom.

Your inner restoration will not come from your strength, but through the truth you plant in your mind. Fill yourself with the Word. Surround yourself with truth. And when doubt comes, respond with faith.

Prayer
Father, thank You for giving me Your Word that cleanses, restores, and transforms. Help me renew my mind with Your truth. Teach me to tear down the thoughts that don't come from You and embrace what You say about me. Let me think like Christ and walk in obedience to Your will each day. In the name of Jesus Christ,
Amen.

Day 27: Notes

Date: _____

_____

_____

_____

_____

_____

_____

_____

_____

_____

_____

_____

_____

_____

_____

Live in Holiness Intentionally

Holiness is not an unreachable standard reserved for a few. It is a call for all of us, and it begins with an intentional decision to live for God. "But like the Holy One who called you, be holy yourselves also in all your behavior." (1 Peter 1:15) Living in holiness does not mean being perfect. It means being set apart for the Lord. It is recognizing that we were bought at a price and that our lives no longer belong to us. "For you have been bought for a price. Therefore, glorify God in your body." (1 Corinthians 6:20)

Holiness begins in the heart, but it doesn't stay there. It is reflected in our choices, our words, our priorities, and even in what we consume, what we share, and what we tolerate. The world will tell you to follow your heart. The Word calls you to deny yourself and follow Christ. It's not easy, but it is possible when you surrender completely to Him. "Therefore, having these promises, beloved, let's cleanse ourselves from all defilement of flesh and spirit, perfecting holiness in the fear of God." (2 Corinthians 7:1)

Living in holiness requires intention. It doesn't happen by accident. It is saying yes to God every day and no to whatever contaminates the soul. It is guarding what you listen to, what you allow into your mind, and who you let speak into your identity. Being holy is not about living in fear of sinning. It is about living with passion to please the One who rescued you.

And even if you fall, His grace is available to lift you, correct you, and continue forming you into the image of His Son. Inner restoration also means living with a clean heart, being sensitive to His voice, willing to obey and persevere.

Prayer
Father, thank You for calling me to a holy life. Help me live each day intentionally for You, recognizing that I was bought at a price and that my body, mind, and heart belong to You. Cleanse me with Your Word, and help me grow in holiness, not for appearances, but out of love and reverence for You. In the name of Jesus Christ, Amen.

Day 28: Notes

Date: _____

_____

_____

_____

_____

_____

_____

_____

_____

_____

_____

_____

_____

_____

Spiritual Growth

Embrace Silence as Spiritual Training

We live in a world saturated with noise. Opinions, notifications, conversations, everything competes for our attention. But God does not compete with noise. He speaks in a gentle whisper; in that quiet space we often avoid because it confronts us with who we are and with what He wants to say. Silence is not the absence of God. It is the training ground where we learn to recognize His voice. Jesus Himself withdrew to quiet places to pray and be in communion with the Father. (Luke 5:16).

If the Son of God needed silence, how much more do we?
Our minds resist silence. They get restless, distracted, and agitated. That is why we need strategies to focus only on God. One effective way is to pray out loud. Hearing our own words engages our senses and directs our hearts. Another way is to write our prayers as letters to the Lord. When we write, we often open our hearts with deeper honesty. And in every moment, we take every thought captive to the obedience of Christ. (2 Corinthians 10:5).
The soul needs silence to align with heaven. At first, it may feel uncomfortable. You might feel the urge to do something. But if you persevere, you'll begin to hear what you couldn't hear before, not just God's direction, but also the healing He wants to bring.
"But when you pray, go into your inner room, close your door, and pray to your Father who is in secret, and your Father who sees what is done in secret will reward you." (Matthew 6:6)

Make silence a discipline. Not as a burden, but as a sacred appointment. Turn off the noise, close the door, and open your heart. There, in the secret place, God is waiting for you.

Prayer
Father, teach me to embrace silence as a gift from You. Help me stop fearing what is quiet, simple, and hidden. May I not hear my anxiety in the silence, but hear Your voice. Make me a woman who not only prays but also listens with reverence. Help me take control of my thoughts, bring them into obedience to Christ, and build habits that draw me closer to You. I want to seek You with intention, listen to You with attention, and surrender to Your guidance with humility. In the name of Jesus Christ,
Amen.

Day 29: Notes

Date: _____

_____

_____

_____

_____

_____

_____

_____

_____

_____

_____

_____

_____

_____

Share Your Testimony Without Fear

Your story matters. Not because it is perfect, but because in the middle of it is the power of God. Every tear, every fall, every moment of restoration carries the mark of Christ's love. Your testimony is not just a memory from the past. It is a living tool that the Lord wants to use to set others free.

The enemy will try to make you believe that your story is irrelevant, shameful, or too simple. But God says otherwise. In His Kingdom, what has been healed becomes a source of healing. What seemed broken is used to build. And what was once a wound becomes an open door to minister to others.

You don't need to have lived something "spectacular" to have a powerful testimony. If you have passed from death to life, if Jesus found you and rescued you, then you have a story worth telling. And someone is waiting to hear it.
"And they overcame him because of the blood of the Lamb and because of the word of their testimony, and they did not love their life even when faced with death." (Revelation 12:11)

Share what God has done in you. Do it with humility, but with conviction. You don't need the perfect words. You just need to obey. You may not see the fruit right away, but your testimony can be the seed someone else needs to run into the Father's arms.
Silence may feel safer, but obedience brings freedom. Fear cannot silence what God's love has transformed.

Prayer
Lord, give me the courage to share what You have done in my life. Break every fear, shame, and insecurity that tries to keep me quiet. Help me speak with grace, truth, and compassion, knowing that my story can be used by You to touch hearts. May I never forget the miracle You did in me, and may I always be ready to testify of Your faithfulness. In the name of Jesus Christ,
Amen.

Day 30: Notes

Date: _____

_____

_____

_____

_____

_____

_____

_____

_____

_____

_____

_____

_____

_____

_____

Activate a Mountain-Moving Faith

Faith is not passive. It is not just a nice idea or an emotion we feel in hard times. True faith is active. It shows up in decisions, in obedience, in perseverance, and in words that confess who God is, even when we don't see what we're hoping for. It's not about denying reality. It's about declaring with conviction that God is greater than any circumstance. Jesus said that if we had faith the size of a mustard seed, we could say to a mountain, "Move from here to there," and it would move. (Matthew 17:20)

Not because we have power in ourselves, but because we trust in the One who holds all power. A small faith placed in a great God can shake hell itself. But often our faith lies dormant. We talk about trusting, but we still act out of fear. We pray, but we don't move. We hope for miracles, but we don't take steps of obedience. To activate faith means to take risks, move forward, obey even when we don't understand, and declare God's Word above what our natural eyes can see.

The kind of faith that pleases God is the one that stands firm even without visible signs. It does not give up when answers are delayed. It keeps sowing, even when there is no fruit yet. Living faith does not wait to feel something. It acts because it knows in whom it has believed. "Therefore I say to you, all things for which you pray and ask, believe that you have received them, and they will be granted to you." (Mark 11:24)

Today, God is calling you to awaken and activate that faith. Some mountains will only move when you dare to believe, speak, and obey with authority in the name of Jesus.

Prayer
Lord, awaken in me a faith that is active and alive. Help me to believe not only with words but with actions. Teach me to trust when I cannot see, to walk when I don't understand, and to declare Your truth above my circumstances. Let me live each day by faith and not by sight. Use my faith, even if it is small, to move mountains and glorify Your name. In the name of Jesus Christ,
Amen.

Day 31: Notes

Date: _____

_____

_____

_____

_____

_____

_____

_____

_____

_____

_____

_____

_____

Respond When He Calls You by Name

God doesn't call in crowds. He calls by name. He doesn't see you as just another face in the crowd. He sees you as His daughter, loved and chosen. His calling is personal, intentional, and full of purpose. "Samuel, Samuel..." And he said, 'Here I am.'" (1 Samuel 3:4)

When God calls, it's not just to assign a task. His call is, above all, an invitation to intimacy. He calls to speak to you, to transform you, and to use you for His glory. God called Samuel when he was young, in the stillness of the night, when everyone else was asleep.

In the same way, God still calls today, amid the noise, the routine, the exhaustion, and our distractions. And just like Samuel, many times we don't recognize His voice right away. But the more time we spend with Him, the more we learn to discern His direction.

Responding to God's call won't always be comfortable. It may mean stepping out of your safe zone, making bold decisions, or letting go of your plans. But when you say, "Yes, Lord," you are aligning your life with His eternal will. You're saying, "Not my will, but Yours be done."

Sometimes God calls to send you. Other times, to correct you. And many times, simply to be with you. Don't ignore His voice. Don't delay your response. The One who calls you by name is the same One who created you with a purpose. When He calls, He does it with love, clarity, and a perfect plan.

Are you willing to say, like Samuel, "Speak, Lord, for Your servant is listening"? That response could change everything.

Prayer
Lord, thank You for calling me by name. Even though I've often been distracted or afraid, today I want to respond with a willing heart. Open my ears to recognize Your voice, and give me the courage to obey without delay. Let my entire life be a continual response to Your call. In the name of Jesus Christ, Amen.

Day 32: Notes

Date: _____

_____

_____

_____

_____

_____

_____

_____

_____

_____

_____

_____

_____

_____

Break Free from the Past Once and for All

There are chains you can't see, but you can feel their weight. The past, with its mistakes, wounds, decisions, and sins, can become an invisible prison that steals your joy, hope, and purpose. But in Christ, you are not called to carry that weight forever. You are called to live truly free. "Therefore, if anyone is in Christ, this person is a new creation; the old things passed away; behold, new things have come." (2 Corinthians 5:17)

Maybe you've wondered if God forgave you. Maybe you've confessed the same thing a thousand times, but you still feel guilt and shame. Let me remind you of this: God's forgiveness is not partial. It is complete. It's not based on what you can do, but on what Christ already did on the cross. "As far as the east is from the west, so far has He removed our wrongdoings from us." (Psalm 103:12)

The enemy wants to use your past to hold you back. But God wants to heal it and move you forward. He not only forgives, but He also restores, cleanses, transforms, and gives purpose. Every wound you've experienced can become a platform for His glory if you place it in His hands. Letting go of the past doesn't mean denying what happened. It means surrendering the pain to God, allowing Him to heal you, and choosing to stop reliving what He has already buried. It's walking with your eyes on Christ instead of on what's behind you.

Today, take that step. Let go of the past. Embrace freedom. Live as the woman God has already declared free.

Prayer
Father, today I choose to let go of every weight from my past. I no longer want to live tied to what You have already forgiven. Fill me with Your truth and help me walk in the freedom You've given me. Restore my soul, heal my heart, and use me for Your glory. In the name of Jesus Christ,
Amen.

Day 33: Notes

Date: _____

_____

_____

_____

_____

_____

_____

_____

_____

_____

_____

_____

_____

_____

Stop Comparing Yourself, You Are Unique in Him

Comparison is a silent trap that steals joy, distorts identity, and weakens faith. Our culture constantly pushes us to measure ourselves against others: their success, appearance, achievements, and spirituality. But the Lord did not call you to be a copy. He created you uniquely, with intentional design, your voice, and a specific purpose. "I will give thanks to You, for I am fearfully and wonderfully made" (Psalm 139:14).

God does not make mistakes. When He formed you, He did it with detail, love, and purpose. Every part of your personality, every experience you've lived, and even your weaknesses, can be used by Him to reflect His glory in a way no one else can. If you spend your life wishing for someone else's assignment, you will miss the fullness of what God wants to do through you.

Comparison often comes from insecurity and pride in disguise. We think we are worth more if we do more, look better, or stand out. But in the Kingdom of God, value is not earned. It is received. And you have already been accepted, called, equipped, and loved by the Father.

Today, stop looking around and start looking up. Do not compare yourself, because you are not in competition with anyone. You are in process. The goal is not to become like other women but to become like Christ. And that happens when you walk in obedience, gratitude, and fullness.

Prayer
Father, forgive me for the times I've compared myself to others, forgetting that You created me with purpose. Help me embrace my identity in You and trust that You have given me everything I need to fulfill Your will. I want to live in fullness, without comparisons, and with my eyes fixed only on You. In the name of Jesus Christ, Amen.

Day 34: Notes

Date: _____

_____

_____

_____

_____

_____

_____

_____

_____

_____

_____

_____

_____

_____

Take Refuge in the Presence of God

The presence of God is not a symbolic or distant concept. It is real, powerful, and available to you today. In a world where everything changes, where external noise and inner chaos threaten to overwhelm us, His presence is the only place where we find true peace, direction, and comfort. "He who dwells in the shelter of the Most High will abide in the shadow of the Almighty" (Psalm 91:1).

Taking refuge in God is not a sign of weakness but of wisdom. It recognizes that there are battles we cannot fight alone, burdens we should not carry, and answers that can only be found at the Father's feet. You do not need a perfect place or a special moment. You can run to His presence in the middle of tears, routine, exhaustion, or confusion. He is always available.

When you choose to take refuge in His presence, your soul finds rest. Not because your circumstances change immediately, but because you know you are safe. His peace guards your mind, His Word guides your steps, and His love covers your wounds. He is not a distant God. He is a close Father who invites you to be with Him.

Sometimes we search for answers when what we need most is His presence. You do not always have to say or do much. Sometimes, you just need to be. Worship. Listen. Breathe deeply and remember that He is with you.

Today, do not run to a thousand distractions seeking temporary relief. Take refuge in what is eternal. Run into His arms and stay there.

Prayer
Father, thank You for inviting me to take refuge in Your presence. Help me stop running to superficial things and seek rest only in You. May I find in Your closeness each day the strength, peace, and direction my soul needs. In the name of Jesus Christ,
Amen

Day 35: Notes

Date: _____

Spiritual Power

Practice Disciplines That Strengthen You

Spiritual strength does not appear by accident. It is cultivated. Just as the body needs exercise and nourishment to remain strong, the soul needs disciplines that align it with God's will and prepare it to persevere through trials. "Discipline yourself for the purpose of godliness, for bodily training is only of little profit, but godliness is profitable for all things" (1 Timothy 4:7–8).

Reading the Word, praying, fasting, gathering with other believers, worshiping, and serving are not empty routines. They are life-giving practices that shape you, cleanse you, and draw you closer to the Father's heart. These disciplines do not make you more loved by God, but they do make you more sensitive to His voice and better equipped to live in victory. Jesus said, "The spirit is willing, but the flesh is weak" (Matthew 26:41), which is why we must remain watchful and spiritually nourished.

Do not wait until you are in crisis to strengthen your spirit. Spiritual training is daily, consistent, and sometimes uncomfortable. It is always necessary. Prayer connects you. The Word nourishes you. Fasting sets you free. Fellowship encourages you. Service teaches you how to love. These are not religious rituals. They are tools for growth.
"Abide in Me, and I in you" (John 15:4). When you discipline your spiritual life, you are saying, "My flesh does not lead. The Spirit does." You are building deep roots that will hold you firm when the storm comes. "The wise man built his house on the rock... and it did not fall, for it had been founded on the rock" (Matthew 7:24–25).

Today, ask yourself: What disciplines do I need to recover or strengthen? It is not about doing more, but about doing it with intention. God wants to strengthen you from within, but you must be willing to show up.

Prayer
Lord, help me cultivate a firm and disciplined spiritual life. Show me which habits I need to restore and which distractions I should leave behind. Give me passion for Your presence, hunger for Your Word, and consistency to grow every day. Strengthen me from deep within. In the name of Jesus Christ,
Amen.

Day 36: Notes

Date: _____

Guard Your Heart from Every Distraction

The heart is valuable. It is the center of your emotions, thoughts, desires, and decisions. That is why the Bible calls us to guard it above all else. If we allow it to be filled with noise, anxiety, or misdirected desires, we will quickly lose focus and passion for God.
"Watch over your heart with all diligence, for from it flow the springs of life" (Proverbs 4:23).

Now more than ever, distractions are everywhere. While not all of them are bad in themselves, many become silent enemies of our communion with God. Excessive time on social media, the constant need for validation, comparisons, multitasking, and information overload can harden our hearts or make them shallow.
Jesus warned, "Where your treasure is, there your heart will be also" (Matthew 6:21). This is why we must ask ourselves: Where are we placing our treasure each day?

Guarding the heart means taking pauses, setting boundaries, and cultivating habits that keep you connected to the Father. It is not about living disconnected from the world but about learning to discern what is pulling you away from God's purpose.
"Test yourselves to see if you are in the faith" (2 Corinthians 13:5).

Make space for silence, for the Word, and prayer. Be careful with what you consume, what you repeat in your mind, and what you allow into your soul.
Remember that God is not looking for perfect hearts but for surrendered hearts, hearts that are moldable and willing to obey.
"Blessed are the pure in heart, for they shall see God" (Matthew 5:8).

Today, choose to guard your heart with care. Not because you are weak, but because you know that your spiritual strength is cultivated there.

Prayer
Father, give me wisdom to guard my heart as You have commanded. Deliver me from the distractions that pull me away from You, and show me what I need to adjust in my daily life. May my heart always be fertile ground for Your truth. In the name of Jesus Christ, Amen.

Day 37: Notes

Date: _____

_____

_____

_____

_____

_____

_____

_____

_____

_____

_____

_____

_____

_____

Be an Active Part of the Body of Christ

Following Christ is not an individualistic experience. You were designed to live out your faith in community, as part of a body where every member has an essential role. You are not alone, and you were not called to walk alone. You are part of something much greater than yourself: the body of Christ. "So we, who are many, are one body in Christ, and individually parts of one another" (Romans 12:5).

Every woman in the church has a specific purpose. Some teach, others encourage, and others serve quietly. All are valuable. When you understand this, you stop competing and begin to collaborate. You stop comparing and start contributing. "But to each one is given the manifestation of the Spirit for the common good" (1 Corinthians 12:7). Being an active part of the body of Christ does not mean being busy all the time. It means being available for what God wants to do in and through you. Isolating yourself might feel more comfortable, but it weakens you spiritually. Fellowship with other believers sharpens you, builds you up, and protects you.

"Iron sharpens iron, so one person sharpens another" (Proverbs 27:17). You need the wisdom of other women, their support in the battle, their loving correction, and their sincere prayers. And they need you too. Participating actively requires commitment, humility, and a willing heart. You may feel unqualified or think you have nothing to offer, but if the Holy Spirit lives in you, you have everything you need to be a blessing. "For we are His workmanship, created in Christ Jesus for good works" (Ephesians 2:10).

Do not stay isolated. Get involved. Pray with others, serve with joy, and build up with your words. When you choose to be an active part of the body, not only do you grow, but the whole body is strengthened.

Prayer

Lord, thank You for making me part of Your body. Help me live in community with my brothers and sisters in Christ, with humility and willingness. Show me where and how I can serve, and free me from isolation or pride. I want to be a living, useful, and obedient part for Your glory. In the name of Jesus Christ,
Amen.

Day 38: Notes

Dates: _____

_____

_____

_____

_____

_____

_____

_____

_____

_____

_____

_____

_____

_____

_____

Do Not Improvise: Seek the Anointing with Commitment

In the Kingdom of God, it is not all about talent, charisma, or good intentions. What truly makes a difference in a life of impact is the anointing of the Holy Spirit. But anointing is not improvised. It is cultivated through commitment, obedience, intimacy, and a surrendered life. "But You have exalted my horn like that of the wild ox; I have been anointed with fresh oil" (Psalm 92:10).

Anointing is not emotion. It is divine backing. It is the evidence that God is behind what you are doing. And although the Spirit is the One who gives it, you are responsible for protecting the oil.
"Not by might nor by power, but by My Spirit," says the Lord of armies (Zechariah 4:6). You cannot walk in spiritual authority if your relationship with God is shallow or inconsistent.
Many times, we want results without process, visibility without preparation, and power without prayer. But God is not impressed by appearances. He anoints those who are willing to pay the price in secret.

"Your Father who sees in secret will reward you" (Matthew 6:6).
He anoints those who say "yes" when it is hard, "no" when it is necessary, and "here I am" when they feel unqualified.
If God has given you an assignment, do not improvise. Prepare yourself. Fill your heart with His Word. Pray without ceasing. Fast. Walk in holiness. Serve with integrity. The anointing is not only for the pulpit. It is for raising children, leading, working, counseling, and living with purpose.
"Be devoted to prayer" (Romans 12:12).
Where there is commitment, there is fresh oil.

Today, examine your heart. Are you cultivating a life God can anoint? Do not improvise. Seek the anointing with commitment.

Prayer
Lord, I do not want to do anything in my strength. I want Your anointing over my life. Help me live with commitment, protect the oil You have given me, and remain faithful in the secret place. May every step I take be backed by Your presence. In the name of Jesus Christ,
Amen.

Day 39: Notes

Date: _____

_____

_____

_____

_____

_____

_____

_____

_____

_____

_____

_____

_____

Walk with Eternal Purpose

You were not created to live aimlessly. Your life has direction, purpose, and eternity in mind. God did not save you just so you could survive day by day, but so you could live with focus, leaving a legacy that goes beyond this world. "Set your minds on the things above, not on the things that are on earth" (Colossians 3:2).

Eternal purpose does not always look big in the eyes of the world. Sometimes it shows up in small acts: parenting with patience, serving with love, speaking a word of encouragement, and standing firm when no one else does. But each of those actions, when done in faith and obedience, carries eternal value. "Therefore, my beloved brothers and sisters, be firm, immovable, always excelling in the work of the Lord, knowing that your labor is not in vain in the Lord" (1 Corinthians 15:58).

Walking with eternal purpose means living with the awareness that everything matters. Your decisions today are building your legacy and affecting generations. You are not here by accident but for a divine mission. That mission is not measured by visible accomplishments but by daily faithfulness. "For we are His workmanship, created in Christ Jesus for good works, which God prepared beforehand so that we would walk in them" (Ephesians 2:10).

The enemy wants you to live distracted, discouraged, or trapped in the temporary. But the Holy Spirit wants to awaken you to the eternal. When you live with your eyes fixed on Christ, your priorities shift. What once seemed urgent no longer is. And what once seemed insignificant becomes sacred. "Fix your eyes on Jesus, the author and perfecter of faith" (Hebrews 12:2).

Today is a good day to realign your walk. Ask yourself: Does what I'm doing have eternal value? Am I investing my time in what truly lasts?

Prayer
Father, thank You for giving me a life with purpose. Help me live each day with my eyes set on what is eternal. Free me from distraction and meaningless routine. May everything I do be led by Your Spirit and aligned with Your will. In the name of Jesus Christ,
Amen.

Day 40: Notes

Date: _____

_____

_____

_____

_____

_____

_____

_____

_____

_____

_____

_____

_____

_____

Let His Power Be Perfected in Your Weakness

How many times have you felt like you are not strong enough to keep going? Maybe you are facing a situation that overwhelms you, an emotion you cannot control, or a burden that is wearing you out. But instead of hiding your weakness or trying to overcome it in your own strength, what if you offered it to God? The apostle Paul left us with a powerful truth: "My grace is sufficient for you, for power is perfected in weakness" (2 Corinthians 12:9).

This is not an invitation to give up in defeat but to surrender with purpose. It is in your most fragile moments that God's power is revealed most clearly. Not because you can, but because He can. When you acknowledge your need for Him, His grace surrounds you. His power begins to work not in spite of your weakness but through it. "He gives strength to the weary, and to the one who lacks might He increases power" (Isaiah 40:29).

True spiritual strength does not come from pride or self-sufficiency but from a surrendered life that declares, "Lord, I cannot do this without You."

Stop hiding what makes you vulnerable. Cry if you need to. Ask for help. But above all, come before God just as you are and allow His power to do what you cannot do on your own.
"Call to Me, and I will answer you" (Jeremiah 33:3).
He is not shocked by your weakness, He redeems it.

Today, instead of forcing yourself to be strong, offer your limitations to the Lord. In your weakness, He will be glorified.

Prayer
Father, I recognize there are areas in my life where I feel weak and unable. Today, I do not want to hide them or face them alone. I give them to You so that Your power may be perfected in me. Strengthen me with Your grace and do in me what only You can do. In the name of Jesus Christ,
Amen.

Day 41: Notes

Date: _____

Let Brokenness Transform You

Brokenness is not something we seek, but it is something God can use powerfully. When everything seems to fall apart, when what held you up is no longer there, when your heart is in pieces, that is exactly where God wants to work. Not to destroy you, but to rebuild you with an eternal purpose. "The sacrifices of God are a broken spirit; a broken and a contrite heart, God, You will not despise" (Psalm 51:17).

In a culture that exalts self-sufficiency, God draws near to the brokenhearted. The kind of brokenness that humbles you also brings you closer to His presence. "The Lord is near to the brokenhearted and saves those who are crushed in spirit" (Psalm 34:18).

You are not broken without purpose. You are in the hands of the Potter. He does not discard the pieces. He gathers them one by one and forms something new, more beautiful, more solid, more surrendered.
Sometimes your strength must break so that you learn to rely completely on His power. "My grace is sufficient for you, for power is perfected in weakness" (2 Corinthians 12:9).

Letting brokenness transform you means allowing God to work deeply within you, to remove what hinders, to heal what hurts, and to cleanse what was hidden. Do not resist the process. Offer Him your pain and say, "Do whatever You need to do in me."

What is born out of brokenness in His hands always brings life. What seemed like a loss in His presence becomes purpose.

Prayer
Father, today I come before You with a broken heart. I no longer want to hide the pain or harden myself to avoid it. Do Your work in me. Transform me from the inside out. Use this brokenness to shape something in me that reflects Your glory. In the name of Jesus Christ, Amen.

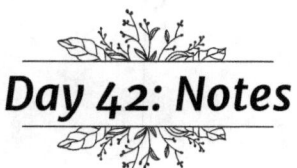

Day 42: Notes

Date: _____

_____

_____

_____

_____

_____

_____

_____

_____

_____

_____

_____

_____

Godly Character

Do Everything with Excellence for Him

Excellence is not perfection. It is not about doing everything without mistakes, but about doing it with a willing heart, with care, and above all, for the glory of God. When you understand that everything you do, even the most ordinary things, can be an act of worship, the way you live begins to change. "Whatever you do, do your work heartily, as for the Lord and not for people" (Colossians 3:23).

Your work, your service, the way you care for your family, your words, and your attitudes can all reflect the God who lives in you. Doing it "as for Him" raises your standard, not out of obligation but out of love. "Whether, then, you eat or drink or whatever you do, do all to the glory of God" (1 Corinthians 10:31).

A godly character does not seek the applause of people but the smile of God. Even in secret, when no one is watching, a surrendered heart strives to act with excellence, knowing that God always sees. "The Lord weighs the spirits" (Proverbs 16:2). And that is enough.

Excellence does not compete, it does not boast, and it does not wear itself out through comparison. It simply gives its best with what it has. Because when everything is done for Him, nothing is small and nothing is in vain. "Let us not become discouraged in doing good, for in due time we will reap, if we do not become weary" (Galatians 6:9).

*Today, examine your attitude and your effort in daily life. Are you doing things with excellence or just trying to get them done? Are you working to please people or to honor the Lord?
Do everything with excellence. Not to be recognized, but because He is worthy of your best.*

Prayer
*Lord, today I want everything I do to be for You. Help me live with excellence, not seeking human approval but desiring to please You in every detail. May even the simplest things become acts of worship. In the name of Jesus Christ,
Amen.*

Día 43: Notas

Fecha: _____

_____

_____

_____

_____

_____

_____

_____

_____

_____

_____

_____

_____

_____

_____

_____

Shine with the Light of Christ Wherever You Are

You do not need a stage or a crowd to make an impact in the world. Sometimes, the most ordinary places, such as your home, your job, the store, or a casual conversation, become platforms to reflect the light of Christ. Not because you are perfect, but because He shines through you. "You are the light of the world. A city set on a hill cannot be hidden" (Matthew 5:14).

Jesus did not say, "Try to be light," but rather, "You are." That is your identity in Him. And where there is light, darkness cannot prevail. "For you were once darkness, but now you are light in the Lord. Walk as children of light" (Ephesians 5:8). To shine does not mean acting religiously or forcing your faith with empty words. It means living with integrity, loving unconditionally, speaking with wisdom, and acting with compassion. It means reflecting the King in every gesture, even the smallest ones.

"Let your light shine before people in such a way that they may see your good works and glorify your Father who is in heaven" (Matthew 5:16). Shining with His light means bringing hope where there is sadness, peace where there is chaos, and truth where there is confusion. Do not underestimate the place where you are today. God did not make a mistake in placing you there. You are exactly where you can make a difference. Sometimes a smile, a word of encouragement, a silent prayer, or a humble act can spark something eternal in someone else's heart.

Today, remember that you are not in the shadows. You are light. And when the light of Christ shines in you, others will see God through your life.

Prayer

Lord, thank You for making me a bearer of Your light. Help me shine right where I am, with what I have, and with who I am. May others see Christ in me, not only through my words, but through every act of love and truth. In the name of Jesus Christ,
Amen.

Day 44: Notes

Date: _____

_____

_____

_____

_____

_____

_____

_____

_____

_____

_____

_____

Surrender Fully to His Will

Surrendering to God's will is not always easy. Sometimes we want to obey, but on our terms. Other times, we say we trust, but we still cling to control. True surrender is not partial or conditional. It is total. It means saying to God, "Do whatever You want, whenever You want, however You want."

Jesus gave us the perfect example of surrender when He prayed: "Father, if You are willing, remove this cup from Me. Yet not My will, but Yours be done" (Luke 22:42). If the Son of God surrendered like that, how could we not do the same?

Surrendering fully does not mean you will always understand what God is doing. It means you will trust His heart. He sees what you cannot see. He knows what you do not know. And if His will leads you down a path you would not have chosen, it is because He knows what is best for your eternal good.

"Trust in the Lord with all your heart, and do not lean on your own understanding" (Proverbs 3:5). Surrender is not a sign of weakness. It is a demonstration of faith. It is the heart that bows down, not just in prayer, but also in obedience.
"It is no longer I who live, but Christ lives in me" (Galatians 2:20).
It means saying to God with sincerity, "Not my will, but Yours be done."

Today is the day to stop negotiating with God. Give Him everything. Do not cling to your plans, your pride, or your fear. Surrender it all to the One who gave everything for you. "The will of God is good and acceptable and perfect" (Romans 12:2).

Prayer

Father, today I surrender my will to Yours. Even if I do not understand everything, I trust that You know what is best for me. Help me release everything that keeps me from obeying with joy. May my life reflect a heart fully surrendered in faith. In the name of Jesus Christ, Amen.

Day 45: Notes

Date: _____

Let Him Heal Your Deepest Wounds

We all carry wounds. Some are visible, others are hidden behind a smile. Some wounds come from rejection, betrayal, loss, or words that left a mark on the soul. But no matter how deep they are, there is no wound that God cannot heal. He is not indifferent to your pain. His Word says: "He heals the brokenhearted and binds up their wounds" (Psalm 147:3).

He not only sees your wound, but He draws near with love, tenderness, and power to restore you completely. "Behold, I will bring healing to you, and I will heal you of your wounds" (Jeremiah 30:17).
Healing is not always immediate. Sometimes it involves remembering, crying, forgiving, and letting go. But the process, when held in His hands, is safe. His purpose is never to expose you to cause more pain, but to set you free. Where you see ruin, He sees the possibility of redemption.

Many times, we try to move on by ignoring the pain, covering it up with busyness, or pretending that everything is fine. But the heart cannot heal unless it is treated with truth and compassion. Today, Jesus extends His hand and says to you, "Show Me your wound. Do not be afraid. I came to heal you."

Do not settle for living wounded. Do not accept an emotionally fragmented life. In Christ, there is complete healing, real restoration, and true freedom. He cannot only heal your pain. He wants to. But He is waiting for you to bring it to Him with a surrendered heart.

Prayer
Father, You know every wound I carry inside. Nothing is hidden from You. Today I choose to open my heart and allow You to heal the deepest areas of my life. Help me trust Your process and give You the pain I have been holding onto. May Your love restore me completely. In the name of Jesus Christ,
Amen.

Day 46: Notes

Date: _____

_____

_____

_____

_____

_____

_____

_____

_____

_____

_____

_____

_____

_____

Believe in the God of the Impossible

True faith is not based on what you see, but on who God is. He is not limited by circumstances, diagnoses, timing, or statistics. Where people say, "It's impossible," His Word declares:
"Is anything too difficult for the Lord?" (Genesis 18:14).

This statement is not just a promise. It is an invitation to lift your eyes and believe. Not in the solution you imagine, but in the God who can do all things according to His perfect will.
"Jesus said to him, 'If you can believe, all things are possible to him who believes'" (Mark 9:23).

God is not asking you for enormous faith but for genuine faith. The kind of faith that says, "I don't understand how, but I know You can." That kind of faith moves mountains, parts the seas, brings life to what is barren, and gives hope amid chaos.

"For we walk by faith, not by sight" (2 Corinthians 5:7).
Not because you make it happen, but because He is faithful.
Maybe you have been praying for something you still have not seen. Maybe you have stopped believing because God's silence has been painful. But today He reminds you: "For nothing will be impossible with God" (Luke 1:37).

Believe again. Trust again.
Faith does not deny reality, but it dares to declare that God has the final word. And that changes everything.

Prayer
Father, today I renew my faith in You. Even if I have not yet seen the answer, I believe that nothing is impossible for You. Help me trust more in Your power than in my circumstances. Increase my faith and teach me to wait with hope, knowing that You are faithful. In the name of Jesus Christ,
Amen.

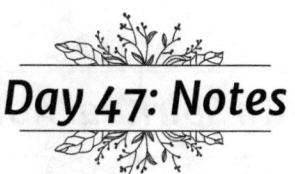

Day 47: Notes

Date: _____

_____

_____

_____

_____

_____

_____

_____

_____

_____

_____

_____

Pray with Spiritual Authority

Prayer is not a passive act. It is a powerful tool God has given us to intervene in the unseen, establish His will on earth, and fight battles in the spiritual realm. We do not pray as beggars hoping for crumbs, but as daughters who know their Father and trust in His power.
"Therefore, let us approach the throne of grace with confidence, so that we may receive mercy and find grace for help at the time of our need" (Hebrews 4:16).

The Word says: "The effective prayer of a righteous person can accomplish much" (James 5:16). It is not about fancy words, repetition, or magic formulas. It is about a surrendered and righteous life, connected to God's heart, praying with faith and authority.
Praying with authority is not about shouting or trying to impress. It is about speaking with the conviction that God hears and responds. It means aligning yourself with His will and declaring His promises above what you see.

"This is the confidence which we have before Him, that if we ask anything according to His will, He hears us" (1 John 5:14).
When you pray according to the Word, you are praying according to His will. You are using the sword of the Spirit, which is the Word of God, to confront the lies of the enemy and declare life, truth, and freedom. Many times, we settle for weak prayers, filled with doubt or fear. But today, God is calling you to pray as someone who knows who she belongs to. Your voice in heaven carries weight when it comes from a surrendered heart filled with His truth.

Rise in faith. Do not repeat what you feel. Proclaim what you believe. Do not pray from a place of defeat. Pray from the victory that Christ has already won.

Prayer
Father, thank You for giving me access to Your presence. Today I pray with faith, with authority, and with the certainty that You hear me. Align my heart with Yours and teach me to pray according to Your Word. May my prayers be effective, fervent, and full of faith. In the name of Jesus Christ,
Amen.

Day 48: Notes

Date: _____

Use His Word as Your Sword

The Christian life is not a casual walk. It is a daily battle, and it is not fought with human weapons, but with spiritual ones. One of the most powerful is the Word of God, called in Ephesians 6:17 "the sword of the Spirit, which is the word of God."

God has given us His Word not just to read or memorize, but to use. In times of temptation, confusion, fear, or pain, the Word is your offensive weapon. You are not defenseless. When you declare God's truth, the enemy cannot stand against it.

"For the weapons of our warfare are not of the flesh, but divinely powerful for the destruction of fortresses" (2 Corinthians 10:4). Jesus Himself gave us the example. When He was tempted in the wilderness, He did not argue or reason. He responded with, "It is written..." and quoted Scripture (Matthew 4). That is the same authority you can use to respond, not with your emotions, but with eternal truth.

But to use the Word as a sword, you need to know it. You cannot fight with what you do not know. That is why you must invest time reading it, meditating on it, and storing it in your heart.
"I have treasured Your word in my heart, so that I may not sin against You" (Psalm 119:11). When the evil day comes, you will not fight from fear, but from conviction.

Do not underestimate the power of declaring God's Word over your thoughts, your family, your decisions, and your battles. When you speak what God says, you align your reality with His will.

Prayer
Lord, thank You for giving me Your Word as my sword. Help me love it, know it, and use it with wisdom. May I not fight in my strength, but with the truth that comes from You. Teach me to declare Your Word with authority in every area of my life. In the name of Jesus Christ, Amen.

Day 49: Notes

Date: _____

_____

_____

_____

_____

_____

_____

_____

_____

_____

_____

_____

_____

_____

_____

Peace and Trust

Seek Restoration, Not Just to Win Arguments

There is a big difference between being right and having your heart in the right place. In a world that rewards those who speak the loudest or win with arguments, God calls us to seek peace, not personal victory. It is not about proving superiority, but about reflecting Christ, even in the midst of conflict. "Blessed are the peacemakers, for they will be called sons of God" (Matthew 5:9).

The Word teaches us: "If possible, so far as it depends on you, be at peace with all people" (Romans 12:18). This does not mean we should never speak firmly or stand up against injustice. It means our desire should always be reconciliation, not confrontation driven by pride.

Winning an argument may feed the ego, but restoring a relationship glorifies God. Sometimes, silence is wiser than a sharp reply. Sometimes, being quiet is not losing, it is loving. And other times, speaking with grace and truth can open doors that anger would only close.

"A gentle answer turns away wrath, but a harsh word stirs up anger" (Proverbs 15:1). Choosing peace does not mean you are weak. It means you trust that God is just and that He is the one who defends the truth. Seeking restoration does not deny conflict. It means facing it with humility and with a desire to reflect Christ more than to defend yourself. "Do not be overcome by evil but overcome evil with good" (Romans 12:21).

Prayer
Father, help me have a heart that seeks peace over pride. Teach me to speak with wisdom, to listen with humility, and to stay silent when needed. In every conversation, may my goal not be to win, but to reflect Your character. Give me a peacemaking spirit that always seeks restoration. In the name of Jesus Christ,
Amen.

Day 50: Notes

Date: _____

_____

_____

_____

_____

_____

_____

_____

_____

_____

_____

_____

_____

_____

Be a Wise and Prudent Woman

Wisdom is not measured by how much you know, but by how you live. A wise and prudent woman is not the one who always speaks, but the one who knows when to be silent, when to act, and above all, when to trust God more than her impulses. "The wise woman builds her house, but the foolish tears it down with her own hands" (Proverbs 14:1).

Wisdom is not just a beautiful quality. It is a spiritual necessity. It is what holds your home, your relationships, your decisions, and your testimony together. "The fear of the Lord is the beginning of wisdom" (Proverbs 9:10). A wise woman does not seek to impress. She seeks to build. She does not react with overwhelming emotions but responds with discernment. She does not make hasty decisions. She seeks God and waits for His direction. And when she makes mistakes, she learns, humbles herself, and grows.

Prudence is her companion. She speaks with intention, acts with purpose, and knows when to step back and pray instead of arguing. In a noisy world, a wise woman is a quiet testimony of Christ's character. "She opens her mouth in wisdom, and the teaching of kindness is on her tongue" (Proverbs 31:26).

We are not born wise, but we can ask the Father, and He gives wisdom generously to those who seek it sincerely.
"But if any of you lacks wisdom, let him ask of God, who gives to all generously and without reproach" (James 1:5).

Wisdom is not out of reach. It is the fruit of the fear of the Lord and a life surrendered to His Word.

Prayer
Father, I long to be a wise and prudent woman who honors You in every area of my life. Help me build and not tear down. Teach me to speak with grace, to act with purpose, and to decide with discernment. Make me sensitive to Your voice and dependent on Your guidance. In the name of Jesus Christ,
Amen.

Day 51: Notes

Date: _____

Love as Christ Loves You

True love does not depend on how others treat you, but on who you belong to. Loving as Christ loves you is not a passing emotion. It is a constant decision. It means loving those who do not deserve it, forgiving those who have failed, and extending grace even when it hurts.

"This is My commandment, that you love one another, just as I have loved you" (John 15:12). Jesus did not give us a suggestion. He gave us a command. His love was sacrificial, patient, faithful, and compassionate. "Love is patient, love is kind, it is not jealous; love does not brag, it is not arrogant" (1 Corinthians 13:4).

Loving like Christ does not mean allowing abuse or injustice, but it does mean your heart remains soft. It means you do not repay evil for evil and that you choose to honor God in the way you treat others.
This kind of love transforms. It restores relationships, heals wounds, and breaks chains of bitterness. It is not based on what you receive, but on what you have already received from Him. "We love, because He first loved us" (1 John 4:19).

And when you love this way, you reflect Christ more powerfully than with a thousand words. Not everyone will appreciate that love. Some may reject it. But it is never in vain. Every act of love, no matter how small, has eternal power when it flows from the heart of God.

Prayer
Lord, thank You for loving me with perfect and constant love. Today I choose to love as You love me, not because of what others do, but because of what You have already done for me. Free me from bitterness and teach me to forgive, to serve, and to bless, even when it is hard. May my life be a faithful reflection of Your love. In the name of Jesus Christ,
Amen.

Day 52: Notes

Date: _____

_____

_____

_____

_____

_____

_____

_____

_____

_____

_____

_____

_____

_____

Cultivate a Gentle Spirit That Stands Firm in Truth

Gentleness is not weakness. It is strength under control. A gentle woman is not someone who allows everything, but someone who chooses to respond with grace, even when she has every reason to react harshly. Gentleness is a powerful virtue when it is paired with firmness in truth. "Blessed are the gentle, for they will inherit the earth" (Matthew 5:5). Jesus was gentle and humble in heart, yet He never compromised the truth. He showed us that it is possible to speak with authority without being aggressive, to correct with love, and to defend truth without losing inner peace. "Learn from Me, for I am gentle and humble in heart, and you will find rest for your souls" (Matthew 11:29). The Bible says: "The wisdom from above is first pure, then peaceable, gentle, reasonable, full of mercy and good fruits, impartial, free of hypocrisy" (James 3:17).

That is the kind of spirit God wants to shape in you.
While many raise their voices to be heard, a woman who is gentle and firm in truth makes a greater impact through her character than through her volume. She does not need to impose, because the truth she lives by speaks for itself. Your adornment must not be merely external... but it should be the hidden person of the heart, with the imperishable quality of a gentle and quiet spirit, which is precious in the sight of God" (1 Peter 3:3–4).
Cultivating this kind of spirit requires daily surrender. It is not always easy to be quiet, to yield, or to speak with kindness. But with the help of the Holy Spirit, you can be courageous and firm without losing compassion.

Do not choose between gentleness and truth as if they were opposites. Embrace both. Being gentle does not mean yielding to error or speaking with hesitation. You can be gentle and, at the same time, firm and clear when proclaiming God's truth. That combination is evidence of spiritual maturity and a powerful testimony.

Prayer
Father, shape in me a spirit like Christ's, gentle, yet firm in truth. Free me from reacting with pride or harshness. Teach me to speak with love, to act with compassion, and to remain steadfast in what Your Word teaches. In the name of Jesus Christ,
Amen.

Day 53: Notes

Date: _____

_____

_____

_____

_____

_____

_____

_____

_____

_____

_____

_____

_____

_____

Live the Fruit of the Spirit Every Day

The fruit of the Spirit is not just a decorative list. It is the evidence of a life surrendered to God. Love, joy, peace, patience, kindness, goodness, faithfulness, gentleness, and self-control (Galatians 5:22–23) are not qualities we produce through human effort. They are manifestations of the Holy Spirit in a life that remains in Him.

It is not about "trying harder," but about surrendering more deeply. The closer you walk with the Lord, the more naturally His character will be reflected in you. Fruit is not forced, it is cultivated. And it is cultivated through prayer, obedience, and daily dependence on God.
"I am the vine; you are the branches. The one who remains in Me, and I in him, bears much fruit, for apart from Me you can do nothing" (John 15:5).

A woman led by the Spirit does not live reactively, but intentionally. She does not respond to circumstances based on her emotions, but from what the Spirit is producing within her. This does not mean perfection. It means transformation.
Each part of the fruit is a powerful tool to impact your home, your relationships, and your surroundings. Love restores. Joy strengthens. Peace calms. Patience sustains. Kindness leads. Self-control protects. And all of this glorifies God.

Living the fruit of the Spirit means living differently. It means carrying the presence of God wherever you go. It is not something that only shows up in "spiritual moments," but in daily life, in difficult conversations, in long seasons of waiting, and in moments of unexpected injustice.

Prayer
Holy Spirit, grow Your fruit in me each day. Help me live surrendered to You so that Your character may be formed in my heart. May love, patience, joy, faith, and every part of the fruit become visible in my life. Let others see You reflected in me. In the name of Jesus Christ, Amen.

Day 54: Notes

Date: _____

Build a Life of Constant Prayer

Prayer is not just talking to God in times of need. It is always living in communion with Him. A life of constant prayer does not mean spending hours in isolation. It means cultivating an ongoing relationship with the Father throughout the day.
"Pray without ceasing" (1 Thessalonians 5:17).

This instruction is not a burden. It is an invitation to stay connected to heaven while walking through life on earth. It means learning to talk to God while you work, cook, drive, or face challenges.
A woman who prays constantly does not live from a place of anxiety but from a place of trust. "Do not be anxious about anything, but in everything by prayer and pleading with thanksgiving, let your requests be made known to God" (Philippians 4:6).

She does not wait for the "perfect moment" to pray. Instead, she has made prayer a daily, natural, and vital habit. She knows that without prayer, her soul grows weak, but with prayer, her faith grows strong. Prayer does not need to be complicated or eloquent. God is not looking for perfection in your words, but sincerity in your heart. You can speak to Him as a daughter who depends on her Father, with confidence, reverence, and love. "The Lord is near to all who call on Him, to all who call on Him in truth" (Psalm 145:18).

Building a life of prayer is an intentional decision. It means giving God the first place in your day, in your decisions, in your burdens, and in your dreams. It also means learning to listen, because prayer is a dialogue, not a monologue.

Prayer
Father, I want to walk with You each day through prayer. Teach me to depend on You in the ordinary moments and to always speak with You. May my heart remain connected to Your presence, and may my life be marked by a constant relationship with You. In the name of Jesus Christ,
Amen.

Day 55: Notes

Date: _____

Manage Your Time with Eternal Intention

Your time is one of the most valuable resources God has given you. Every passing minute will not return. That is why living with eternal intention does not mean simply "doing a lot," but doing what truly matters to God. The Word exhorts us: "So then, be careful how you walk, not as unwise people but as wise, making the most of your time, because the days are evil" (Ephesians 5:15–16).

God does not want you to live in a hurry, but in alignment. Not running without direction, but walking with purpose. A woman who manages her time with wisdom puts God at the center of her schedule. She learns to discern the urgent from the eternal and knows how to say no when something steals her peace or distracts her from her calling. She values her time not by how much she accomplishes, but by how much she obeys.

Living with eternal intention means asking yourself: Is what I am doing honoring God? Is it sowing into the eternal or only into the temporary? It is not about constant productivity, but about having clear priorities. "Commit your works to the Lord, and your plans will be established" (Proverbs 16:3).

The enemy will not always attack you with bad things. Sometimes he will use distractions. That is why you must be intentional. Invest your time in what builds, in what lasts, and in what glorifies God.

Prayer
Father, thank You for the gift of time. Teach me to manage it with wisdom, to make decisions with eternal focus, and to live each day with purpose. May I not be carried away by hurry or superficial things, but seek to please You in every moment. In the name of Jesus Christ, Amen.

Day 56: Notes

Date: _____

_____

_____

_____

_____

_____

_____

_____

_____

_____

_____

_____

_____

_____

_____

_____

Impact and Multiplication

Obey Even When You Don't Understand

Obeying God when everything makes sense is easy. The challenge is to obey when you don't understand why, when the path feels uncertain, or when your logic tells you to go another way. Yet it is in those very moments that faith matures and your obedience brings the greatest glory to God.

The Bible is full of men and women who obeyed without having all the answers. Abraham went out without knowing where he was going. Noah built an ark without ever having seen rain. Mary accepted her calling without fully understanding what it meant. What moved them? Trust in the One who called them. "By faith Abraham, when he was called, obeyed by going out to a place which he was to receive as an inheritance; and he left, not knowing where he was going" (Hebrews 11:8).

Jesus said: "Blessed are those who hear the word of God and follow it" (Luke 11:28). The true blessing is not just in knowing the Word, but in obeying it, even when it is difficult, even when there is no immediate reward. God does not expect you to understand everything. He asks you to trust Him. His will is good, acceptable, and perfect, even when it doesn't seem logical. What you don't understand today may become a testimony tomorrow. And what hurts now may produce eternal fruit later. "Trust in the Lord with all your heart and do not lean on your own understanding" (Proverbs 3:5).

To obey even when you don't understand is not ignorance; it is surrender. It is declaring with your life, "Lord, even if I don't understand the process, I trust in Your will."

Prayer
Father, sometimes I don't understand what You are doing, but today I choose to trust You. Help me obey You without holding back, to walk by faith and not by sight. May my obedience be a true expression of love and complete trust in Your will. In the name of Jesus Christ, Amen.

Day 57: Notes

Date: _____

_____

_____

_____

_____

_____

_____

_____

_____

_____

_____

_____

_____

_____

_____

Receive Peace That Surpasses All Understanding

There is a kind of peace that does not depend on circumstances, on the answers you are waiting for, or on the control you think you have. It is a peace that goes beyond logic, beyond what is humanly possible. It is the peace that only God can give, and it can only be received when you let go of control and trust Him fully.

The Word says: "And the peace of God, which surpasses all comprehension, will guard your hearts and minds in Christ Jesus" (Philippians 4:7). This peace is not fragile. It does not break at the first sign of trouble. It is steady because it comes from heaven.
"You will keep him in perfect peace, whose mind is stayed on You, because he trusts in You" (Isaiah 26:3).

Receiving this peace does not mean denying what you feel. It means surrendering what you feel to the One who reigns over everything. It means saying, "Lord, this hurts, this worries me, but I choose to trust You more than what I see or understand."

When you receive this peace, you are not only sustained, but you also become a source of strength for others. You become a bearer of peace in the midst of chaos, a woman who reflects Christ in the middle of the storm. Your testimony stops being just words and becomes living evidence of God's power.

Do not strive to understand everything. Ask God for His peace. And when you receive it, embrace it with all your heart. That peace will guard your mind, protect your emotions, and give you strength to move forward.

Prayer
Father, today I let go of the need to have everything under control. I give You my thoughts, my fears, and my emotions. Fill me with Your peace, the peace that surpasses all understanding. May that peace guide me, sustain me, and transform me. In the name of Jesus Christ, Amen.

Day 58: Notes

Date: _____

_____

_____

_____

_____

_____

_____

_____

_____

_____

_____

_____

_____

Clothe Yourself with Strength and Dignity

It does not matter what you have been through or how others have defined you. If you are in Christ, you have a new identity. You are a redeemed, loved, set-apart, and equipped woman of God, called to live with purpose. You are not clothed in shame, defeat, or insecurity. You are clothed in strength and dignity. "Strength and dignity are her clothing, and she smiles at the future" (Proverbs 31:25).

This woman is not strong on her own. She is strong because she has been clothed with the character of Christ. She does not smile at the future because she has everything figured out, but because she knows who holds her. "I can do all things through Christ who strengthens me" (Philippians 4:13).

To clothe yourself with strength is to walk with the confidence that God is with you, even when you feel weak. It is rising after a fall, speaking with boldness when there is silence, and continuing to believe when everything seems to be against you.

To clothe yourself with dignity is to remember that you were bought with precious blood. It is to live as a daughter of the King, not as a slave to the past, to fear, or the opinions of others. Your value is not defined by your surroundings, but by the God who called you by name.

Today, choose how you will dress spiritually. Do not pick up the cloak of discouragement or the garments of fear. Put on the armor of God and cover yourself with the identity He has given you. When a woman clothes herself with strength and dignity, everything around her is impacted.

Prayer
Lord, thank You for clothing me with strength and dignity. Today, I renounce every lie that tries to define me and embrace the identity You have given me in Christ. Strengthen my steps, renew my mind, and help me walk as Your daughter. In the name of Jesus Christ, Amen.

Day 59: Notes

Date: _____

_____

_____

_____

_____

_____

_____

_____

_____

_____

_____

_____

_____

_____

Multiply What God Has Given You and Impact Generations

What God has done in your life is not just for you. You were transformed with a greater purpose: to be an active part of the fulfillment of the Great Commission. It is not just about telling your story. It is about making disciples and leading others to know, love, and obey Christ. He said: "Go, therefore, and make disciples of all the nations" (Matthew 28:19).

This command was not only for leaders or missionaries. It was for all of us. You have received by grace, and now you are called to give by grace. Your testimony is a living seed that can awaken faith, restore hearts, and ignite callings. "The things which you have heard from me in the presence of many witnesses, entrust these to faithful people who will be able to teach others also" (2 Timothy 2:2).

You do not need to have all the answers or live a perfect life. You just need to be available and have a surrendered heart. Discipleship is not about impressing. It is about walking with someone, encouraging her, praying for her, sharing the Word, and modeling a life that follows Christ.

Every process you have walked through, every victory you have celebrated, and every wound that God has healed can be used to lift another woman up. Do not keep silent what the Lord has done. Use your story as a key that opens hearts and points others toward Him.

Today is a good day to take the next step. Pray for someone. Call her. Invite her to read the Bible with you. Inspire faith not only with words, but with presence, example, and truth.

Prayer
Lord, thank You for transforming my life. Today, I commit to sharing what I have received by grace. Show me whom I should disciple, how to encourage, and how to sow faith in other women. May my life not only honor You, but also multiply for Your glory. In the name of Jesus Christ,
Amen.

Day 60: Notes

Date: _____

_____

_____

_____

_____

_____

_____

_____

_____

_____

_____

_____

_____

_____

This Is Only the Beginning...

Sixty days of surrender, restoration, formation, and eternal purpose. Sixty days in which the Lord invited you to walk closer, go deeper, and depend more fully on Him.
But this is not the end. This is only the beginning of a truly surrendered life.

Now that His Word has been planted in your heart, it is time to bear fruit. Fruit that remains. Fruit that impacts your family, your church, your friendships, and future generations. God has not raised you up just to sustain you, but to multiply you.

Keep cultivating a life of prayer, obedience, holiness, wisdom, and compassion. Remain firm in the truth, but with a humble heart. And when the voices of fear, doubt, or discouragement try to speak louder, remember what God has already said about you.

Do not go back. Do not live asleep. Do not settle for a superficial faith.

The world needs surrendered women, filled with the Spirit, passionate for Christ, and committed to His mission. Women who inspire, who disciple, who serve, and who love with courage. That woman is you.
Keep moving forward. Keep growing. Keep multiplying what God has done in you.

Because a truly surrendered woman doesn't just change her own story... she changes everything around her.
I bless you in the name of our Lord Jesus Christ,

Leslie Torres
Author

Additional Resources from the Author:

For Women:

SURRENDERED
Lay it all dawn... and know the King like never before
ISBN:979-8-9927393-3-6

Whispers from Heaven
365 Days Prayer Journal to Hear the Voice of God

El Roi: The God Who Sees Me
Finding Freedom in the Desert

Write, Bless, and Prosper
Learn how to publish books that glorify God and earn income from home with Amazon KDP

The Greatest Commandment
What it means and how to live it each day

God's Dream for His Daughters
Discover Your Eternal Purpose in Every Stage of Life

It is important to continue growing and maturing spiritually, but we must not forget the responsibility we have to sow the Word of God into the next generations.
Every child God places in our path is an opportunity to impact the future with faith, love, and truth.
The Jesus' Pinky Promise series is a perfect gift for any special occasion, whether for your own children, grandchildren, nieces, nephews, or any child around you.
Sow eternal seeds today that will bear fruit for a lifetime!

For Children: Jesus' Pinky Promise Series

30 Days of God's Promises for Kids
ISBN: **979-8-9927393-0-5**

*Gratitude Journal
ASIN: B0DZVSLXP7
*Available only on Amazon

Holy Spirit

The Armor of God

Wisdom

Psalms for Worship

www.ingramcontent.com/pod-product-compliance
Lightning Source LLC
Chambersburg PA
CBHW061806120626
46550CB00005B/2160